A Cornish Waif's Story
An Autobiography

A Cornish Waif's Story

An Autobiography

Emma Smith

Introduction by Simon Parker
Foreword by A. L. Rowse

First published in 1954 by Odhams Press Ltd
© 2010 The Estate of Dr A. L. Rowse
Introduction to 2010 edition © Simon Parker

This edition published in 2010 by Truran, Goonance,
Water Lane, St Agnes, Cornwall TR5 0RA

Truran is an imprint of Truran Books Ltd
www.truranbooks.co.uk

ISBN 978 185022 234 7

Front cover illustration:
John Branwell - 'A Street in Newlyn', circa 1890.
From the Branwell Album;
Penlee House, Gallery & Museum, Penzance

Typeset by Kestrel Data, Exeter, Devon

Printed and bound in Cornwall by R. Booth Ltd.,
The Praze, Penryn TR1O 9AA

Contents

Introduction (2010)

A 'MASS OF ILLITERATE RUBBISH' IS HOW NOTED CORNISH academic and historian A L Rowse described the bundle of rough pages brought to him one day by a woman in her sixties, dressed in worn clothes and wearing a head scarf.

What Rowse didn't realise then – and perhaps never quite understood – was that contained in that manuscript was perhaps the most authentic account of late-Victorian child abuse and suffering since Dickens' *A Walk In A Workhouse*.

With hindsight, perhaps, Rowse may have been somewhat jealous of the fact that when *A Cornish Waif's Story* was finally published by Odhams Press in 1954, the reading public was far more interested in the immediacy and honesty of its narrative than in his own scholarly volumes.

Nevertheless, despite his condescending manner and downright rudeness, had it not been for Rowse's presence of mind and hard work, this unique portrait of a poverty-stricken childhood would probably never have seen the light of day.

Published under the nom de plume Emma Smith, it wasn't until many years later that the author's true identity was revealed.

I first became enthralled by the story after picking up a secondhand copy while on holiday in Scotland. Finishing its two hundred or so pages in a single sitting, I was immediately possessed with a determination to find out the 'truth' about 'Emma Smith'. Moreover I felt she deserved far greater recognition.

This quest inevitably led to the door of Trenarren, an imposing granite manor house looking out over St Austell Bay to Gribben Head, and the home of Alfred Leslie Rowse, who was at that time being described by many as 'the greatest living Cornishman'.

Some years earlier, Rowse himself earned plaudits for having discovered Shakespeare's Dark Lady, identifying her as Emilia Lanier. In a sense, I felt it was equally important from a Cornish perspective to reveal the true identity of 'Emma Smith' – Rowse's own 'dark lady'.

Obtaining an invitation to pass through Trenarren's faded portals proved a tortuous affair, involving several false starts and cancelled appointments. But eventually a card arrived in the post, bearing the distinctive 'ALR' moniker and the words 'Come for tea – Thursday at 3'.

Dressed in half-mast trousers, fusty tweed jacket and an expression of unashamed superiority, Rowse cut a comical figure that April afternoon, though their was nothing funny about his demeanour and he made no attempt to play the welcoming host. Clearly in a state of heightened, though unexplained, petulance, my opening question about the author of *A Cornish Waif's Story* resulted in him snapping: "She was a psychotic bitch. I know all about bitches. The woman was ignorant. She was rubbish."

Unbeknown to Rowse, I already knew this to be a grossly inaccurate description of 'Emma Smith'. Long before this meeting, I had undertaken lengthy research, discovering the author of *A Cornish Waif's Story* to be one Mabel Lewis, who chose the nom de plume, Emma Smith, to protect her family.

Born on 24th January 1894, Mabel lived with her grandparents in a row of cottages in St Uny Churchtown, near Redruth, and later at nearby Westharrow, opposite the village shop.

After a traumatic childhood when she was literally sold to a travelling hurdy-gurdy man who treated her abominably, Mabel married an odd-job man she met while incarcerated in a convent. For a short time the couple lived with their three daughters and one son in a crofter's cottage near Aberdeen, before returning to Cornwall, where the children were educated by one Marjorie Probert in Penzance. One of the girls eventually married a clergyman.

More important than establishing Mabel's biographical details, however, was that the research made it possible to state for certain that far from being the "psychotic bitch" described by Rowse, she was regarded highly by all who knew her. For instance, a shopkeeper at St Uny remembered her fondly, telling me: 'She was a very clever woman, a lovely person with a lovely way and a lovely disposition. She could converse well and did so often. She would go out of her way for anyone.'

Rowse, meanwhile, was able to add some detail to the actual process of bringing the book to publication, explaining that he secured the rights over the raw manuscript for a mere £100. He later split the proceeds of the book's sale, giving £375 to Mabel and keeping £425 for himself.

"I managed to make some money for her," he said grudgingly. "We went half-shares, though I had to make a book out of the mass of illiterate manuscripts. It needed a lot of work, cutting it down, dividing it into chapters and paragraphs and the like."

Ultimately, and despite his inexplicably hostile attitude to Mabel Lewis in later years, we have Rowse alone to thank for ensuring this unique account of harrowing poverty, child abuse, misery and degradation was preserved for future generations.

So does the story of Mabel's early life deserve to rank among the most important Cornish books of all time? I think so. *A Cornish Waif's Story* is authentic and accurate, the simple truth of the events described leaving no room for unnecessary embellishment.

It might be argued, with some justification, that Mabel Lewis is no Laurie Lee. And yet what she lacks in poetic, free-flowing prose she more than makes up for in clarity and a childlike honesty.

How many of us, through the fog of intervening adult years, would be capable of recalling and recording with such clarity events which took place when we were barely out of nappies? And for all her lack of literary elegance, Mabel is nevertheless a writer – and one with a rare voice.

What's more, in the course of relating the facts as she remembers them, down to the tiniest detail, she demonstrates her overwhelming and unshakeable ability of seeing the very best in people. Mabel suffered at the hands of her neglectful mother, her cruel step-father, the hurdy-gurdy man and others, yet she still manages to celebrate the moments of light during her childhood. This is an important theme throughout *A Cornish Waif's Story* and perhaps explains why Rowse, who was not famous for his love of simple human nature, didn't quite 'get it'.

Had *A Cornish Waif's Story* been a novel, it would have been well-constructed, neat and satisfying, all the loose ends tied up and cast off with a pleasing denouement. But real life isn't like that; it's untidy and unpredictable, which is what makes Mabel's account so compelling.

Simon Parker
Linkinhorne, Cornwall
Summer 2010

A full account of Simon Parker's encounters with A L Rowse can be found in *Full As An Egg*, also published by Truran

Foreword (1954)

I OWE MY ACQUAINTANCE WITH THIS BOOK, AND ITS AUTHOR,
to the accident of having written A *Cornish Childhood*.
When the manuscript came to me through the post – after
the initial resistance one puts up to unsolicited manuscripts
(for they are rarely any good) – I very soon saw that this was
an exception. Here was a story that held me, fascinated me,
gripped me as no novel could; for it was a true story of life in
the raw – and what a story!

It turned out to be the autobiography of a Cornish girl
– now a woman in her sixties – child of the daughter of a
Cornish miner who had been blinded in a mining accident,
with no means of subsistence. Illegitimate, unwanted, she was
handed over to an organ-grinder with a hide-out in the slums
of Plymouth, with whom she tramped the roads of Cornwall
from Plymouth to Penzance and back again all through
childhood, singing her way through the years during and
after the Boer War at the turn of the century. It was the days
of 'Chase me, Charlie' and 'The Boers have got my Daddy'; of
sweets called Kruger's Whiskers in little country sweet-shops
and when the country's heroes were Roberts and Kitchener.

I used to think of my early circumstances, the restricted
opportunities, the lack of any understanding in a working-
class home, for long with resentment. How much more
reason had this Cornish girl: the stigma of illegitimacy, the

constant feeling of not being wanted, the early years in and out of the workhouse, the searing consciousness of inferiority branded upon a child. Then there was the dirt and indignity of life in a bug-infested Plymouth slum, the separation from her beloved grandparents and the cottage that remained all through the years of restless wandering as an image of security and happiness, a vanished dream to which the child made frantic efforts to find her way back. (Not less so than *le grand Meaulnes* made his despairing attempts to find the road once more to lost bliss.)

But it is the realism, the authentic note of truth that makes this book so impressive and disturbing, and all told so simply and vividly: it is not a book that one can ever forget. I find that its scenes are imprinted naturally and inescapably on the mind – as it might be *Jane Eyre*, so much of which is autobiographical. There are the scenes in the horrible Plymouth tenement-house, with the tame rats treading the wheel in their cage, the shake-down of rags in the corner, the hurdy-gurdy man and his wife reading a newspaper in the feeble lamplight. Or there is the life of fairs and fairgrounds, of the exposure of a girl to the shady company on the roads, the shared barns or lofts or common doss-houses at night. There was the tiredness, the aching feet, the festering sores and blistered heels.

But there were compensations: singing in little Cornish fishing villages in the far west with the flowers bright in cottage gardens, the gulls swooping, or as evening fell with the lights coming out in the windows, along the quayside, the fishing boats at sea. Or there were winter sunsets over the sea, the waves splashing, and the glimpse of firelight in cottage interiors; then the walk back by starlight or the light of the moon playing hide-and-seek with the clouds. And always and everywhere were the native kindness and goodness, the generous hearts of simple people giving what they could, of the little they possessed, to the forlorn, neglected child. Then, too, all the fun of the fairs, of the lions and the circus-girls, of the man on stilts. 'What a wonderful excitement that was, with his wooden legs many, many feet long, and what excitement he caused the next day when he walked down our street tapping on upstair tenement windows, ours included.' 'Come to think of it,' adds our author generously, 'my own children, for all their respectable upbringing, missed some fun.'

I think that shows the right spirit, a good heart, towards such a past. And actually the author tells me that what she would like to do, now in her sixties, is to tramp the length of Cornwall just once more as she did so many times in her childhood.

For, of course, she has made good, though the way has been a hard and an extraordinary one. After running away from the hurdy-gurdy man – a most vivid account, tramping the frost-bound roads of a wintry Cornwall – she finds a refuge in a convent penitentiary; and one has an authentic view of life over the years in such an establishment, to most of us a closed book. After the restlessness and excitement, stillness and peace; after the homelessness, a refuge; after the unwantedness and the sense of shame, tranquillity and love. And through that came the way to the normal life of the world: marriage, children, a home.

Not that those early years have not left their scars: they have inevitably – and these are evident. But what is remarkable is the underlying strength, the toughness, of such a nature – to have come through and made good. Our author is rightly proud of her achievement, and even more of the brother who has risen to good rank as an officer in the Army. It restores one's belief in human nature to come across people who can rise above such circumstances, such handicaps. I thought I knew all about working-class life, the disabilities and handicaps, the disappointments and frustrations; but this book has been a revelation to me. It gives us a unique insight – for I know no other such portrait – into a way of life that is totally unknown to most of us.

A. L. Rowse

Prologue

*Life is like playing a violin solo in public and learning
the instrument as one goes on.*
                    SAMUEL BUTLER.

'HAPPY IS THE MAN (OR WOMAN) WHO HAS NO HISTORY.' NEVER
were truer words spoken than these. I who am about to record
the facts of my own life would give a great deal to be in this
blessed state.

Some time ago a friend who happens to be a sociologist
suggested to me that it might be a good thing if I wrote my
life story. At first I was against the idea. For one thing I have
a mother living who in these latter years I have grown to
love, and the last thing on earth I would wish to do would
be to cause her pain; for, though most of the blame for what
I suffered and endured lies at her door, I have in these latter
years learned to be tolerant and can find many excuses for
her.

My second reason for not agreeing to his proposition at
first was because I argued with myself that even if the record
did no harm, I did not see that it could do good either. It
would not help to reform the conditions under which as a
child I lived and suffered, seeing that many years have elapsed
since then, during which time all sorts of social reforms

have taken place. The child who is the unhappy victim of circumstances and who comes into the world branded with the stigma of illegitimacy, can be, and very often is, adopted into a good home, while others are taken care of in residential nurseries and homes from which much of the old institutional atmosphere has disappeared. In the end, however, I decided that I would make the record, having come to the conclusion that though my story might be too late to do any active good, it was after all a bit of history showing forth the conditions under which some sections of the community existed in the days which are very often referred to as 'the days of plenty', or 'the good old days'.

If my story does nothing else, at least it will cheer the reader to reflect that what I describe in the following pages could not happen in this year of grace 1954.

CHAPTER I

A Workhouse Child

FOR OBVIOUS REASONS AN AUTOBIOGRAPHY SUCH AS I AM about to write must be written under an assumed name. My name then shall be Emma Smith; my place of birth was Redruth in the county of Cornwall.

My very first memories are a vague mixture of my grandmother's tiny cottage in Redruth Church town, and the Workhouse Union a mile or so away. Sometimes I was in one, sometimes in the other. A little brother nearly two years my junior shared my life in both places, though just exactly when he appeared on the scene I cannot tell; I do not remember being without him.

My very first recollection of Harry in the Union is of a small boy who had just been put into his first pair of trousers. A nurse or attendant was proudly holding him by the hand as he stood on a chair, surrounded by an admiring group of children among whom I, as his sister, had pride of place. The attendant waved her hand and started singing 'Three Chairs for the Red, White and Blue'. The youngsters joined in lustily. I left the group and went to find 'three chairs' which I started to drag to the scene of action. Come to think of it, that is not only my first recollection of Harry, but it is the only one as far as life in the Union is concerned.

My memories of him in Grandmother's cottage,

1

however, are much more clear and distinct. He shared my play, he shared my sorrows, he shared my bread and skimmed milk, or kettle broth, and he shared my invariable discontent at meal times; for both of us always whined that the other had the larger quantity, it was in vain that my poor patient grandmother would point out that one or the other had the larger basin, thus explaining the apparent inequality.

One night as Harry and myself were lying side by side in the little nest that our grandmother used to make for us in the corner of the one and only bedroom floor, we heard an unfamiliar voice downstairs in the living-room. We heard our own names. 'I've brought some sweets for Emma and Harry,' said the voice, then after some conversation that I did not catch or perhaps understand, I heard the voice again: 'I met Cod Murphy in the town; he gave me threepence each for Emma and Harry.' Harry by this time was fast asleep, but, sleepy though I was, I strained every nerve to keep awake. I was so excited with the unfamiliar buzz of conversation below, the mention of our names, and the promise of sweets, for sweets were a rare treat to Harry and me.

Presently a heavy step sounded on the stairs and someone entered the room, and in the darkness a woman crept over to our corner. My heart beat wildly as a voice whispered loudly, 'Are you awake, Emma?' 'Yes,' I whispered back. The woman then thrust a bag of sweets into my hand, telling me to share them with Harry. This is my first memory of our mother, though it was not until long afterwards that I realized that was the relationship between us.

My recollections of the Union are made up of incidents that stand out clearly in my mind. There are two occasions that I particularly remember. When I have suffered for some childish crime, I have never been able to remember my crime, but I certainly remember the punishments. Once the Master came up quietly behind me as I sat at table and gave me a box on the ear which sent me spinning backwards off the form on to the floor.

I can strongly recall another occasion when I had been locked out in the yard by myself. There was a wonderful sunset; the red sky seemed to me to be part of home and my grandmother's cottage. Great heaving sobs shook my body as the tears rolled down my cheeks. With my fist stuck into my open mouth – 'Ma!' I kept calling between each sob. I was, I remember, facing the direction of the cottage. I am now several years the wrong side of sixty, yet even now a sky like the one I beheld that evening will take me back to that scene.

One very happy incident I remember that ended in childish tragedy.

The children at the Union were to be taken for a day to the nearest seaside. We were going in brakes, and on that one occasion we were to be dressed in flowery frocks. How thrilled I was with the flowers on my dress, how I loved the excitement of the ride in the brake! Somehow I came in possession of a penny, and I have never forgotten the thrill it gave me as I looked at the different stalls on the beach while clutching my precious coin, to think that I was in the position to purchase some of the delectable goods spread out to tempt the holiday-maker, for in my ignorance there was no limit to what a penny would buy. No housewife even in these difficult days, could spend more thought and care on the spending of a pound than I did on the spending of that penny as I went from stall to stall.

A stout red-cheeked woman dressed in a sunbonnet and clean white apron held out a rosy apple towards me invitingly. I decided this should be my first purchase. I took the apple and at once got my teeth into its luscious flesh as I offered the woman my precious penny and waited expectantly for the change. The woman took no further notice of me, however, so I finished my apple in silence, then sucking my finger thoughtfully I approached the stall-holder and asked her very politely if I might now have my change please. What that female said about kids in general and workhouse bastards in particular I cannot remember. I do remember that she terrified me. Not only was my capital gone, but the smiling world had turned into a very ugly place.

My last memory of the Union is a mixture of excitement and pain. The Master tapped on the window for me as we were at play. On entering the house I was informed that my mother had come to fetch me out. I nearly tripped over myself in my excitement as I was led to the room where my mother was waiting. My face fell as I beheld the young woman I had grown to know slightly as my big sister Maud, for I had expected to see my grandmother whom I had always known as 'Ma'. I brightened up, however, on being assured that I was going home to 'Ma'. My mother started to put a pair of boots on to my feet. They were at least two sizes too small. 'Push your foot in,' she urged impatiently. I tried and tried but no, I could not get my foot in.

'Kick your toe up against the wall,' said Maud, now exasperated. I kicked and kicked, and at last I managed to get those boots on. All the pleasure and excitement of going home to see 'Ma' was completely over-shadowed by the excruciating torture of that walk. When at last we reached Church Town I managed to run to the cottage door where a beloved figure in a clean white apron was shielding her eyes from the sun as she gazed expectantly along the road. Another moment and I was in her arms. Soon I was sitting on my grandfather's knee nestling my head in his jacket, while he puffed contentedly at the familiar clay pipe and remarked in between each puff on my increase in weight since last I sat there. As was his habit he felt my face, then my shoulders, then the size of my feet, to find out how much I had grown, for my beloved grandfather had been robbed of his sight many years before and had never seen any of his children, or their children.

Harry once again figures in my memory. In spite of what

I have said previously, we must have been parted when I was last placed in the Union, for I was certainly alone at the time my mother last fetched me and I had the crippling walk home in the tiny shoes.

It is time I explained a little about my grandparents. My grandfather at the time of their marriage had been a tin-miner, when a little before his eldest child was born he had been the victim of an explosion in the mine which robbed him of his sight. One child after another was born, the number all told exceeding twenty. My mother was the eldest of the family, and when quite a small child had to work on the surface of the mine. Only three girls besides my mother survived infancy, and one brother. My grandfather had no pension, so that the family existed in great poverty; though the poor blind man earned what he could by carting round sand, which in those days housewives used to sprinkle on the stone floors of their kitchens. One or other of his children would lead the pony.

The cottage in which the family lived in my infancy consisted of two rooms, one up, one down. I have no memory at all of sleeping arrangements except the shakedown on the floor which I shared with my little brother.

The living-room was small but cosy and well kept. The cooking stove was bright and shining. What furniture the room contained was good. A large mahogany chest of drawers stood on one side of the room, on the top of which stood a wonderful pair of chandeliers; at least they seemed wonderful to me, for I would naturally notice these things much more after a period in the Union than a child who was always at home. My mother still possesses the chest of drawers, which gleams as richly now as when I first became conscious of it. The knobs on the drawers are inlaid with mother-of-pearl. Sand covered the living-room floor. This would be swept up each day after the morning's cooking, etc., was over, and fresh sand sprinkled down. Grandfather always sat in a polished armchair. The Windsor chairs which stood against the wall under the window likewise gleamed.

Yet though the chairs were free from dust and highly polished, I remember that my aunts would lift the skirts of their best gowns and sit in their petticoats of a Sunday, just in case one tiny speck of dust remained. A grandfather clock ticked solemnly in one corner of the room. This clock was wound and set right from time to time by Grandfather himself in spite of his blindness.

Grandfather figures in many of my happiest memories of early days. As Harry and I sat on his knees he would sing simple folk songs to us in order to keep us good and happy.

The dear man would mend the family boots. I can picture him now with the leg of the iron foot stuck between his knees as he sat in his armchair by the fire. His mouth would be full of nails. This was a never-failing source of wonder to me, for the nails all seemed to be lost in his whiskers, and I could never understand how it was he could find them. I would stand with my hands on his knees gazing up in wonder at him.

I am sure such simple things would have been forgotten long ago if I had had an ordinary childhood, but it was the contrast between these simple homely sights and my other life at the Union that has so firmly embedded them in my mind, and with such affection.

The mantelshelf contained a pair of china ornaments: a lady and gentleman on black and white horses. A large picture of Queen Victoria hung over the mantelpiece, and on the wall opposite the window were a pair of brightly coloured pictures – Daniel in the lions' den and the infant Moses in the bulrushes with Pharaoh's beautiful daughter bending concernedly over him.

A thin leather strap hung near the stove. This was in some way meant to ensure good behaviour on the part of Harry and me. I am sure the strap was never used.

My grandmother made a little money by making herb-beer which she bottled in stone bottles and placed in the window. Pickled onions and marinated fish[1] were also her specialities, and were much appreciated by neighbours who were able to purchase these delicacies from her in small quantities.

The whitewashed bedroom had a few cardboard texts on the walls. From the small window one had a pleasant view of the trees of the Vicarage garden opposite.

Grandmother's bed stood in the centre of the room, and Harry and myself had a snug nest of a bed made up on the floor between the chimney, which jutted right out into the room, and the wall. The cottage was near the church, and we often went round the churchyard with Grandmother, where she would pause by the graves of old friends. Sometimes on these excursions we picked up sticks for the fire, but never on a Sunday for fear of being taken up to the moon, for Grandmother always said that was what would happen.

My grandmother must have been a wonderful woman to cope for periods with Harry and me, after having had so many children of her own. Looking back over it all in these days, the wonder to me is not that we were periodically placed in the Union, but that we were ever taken out.

My mother had not gone to school, but as I have said before, she was put to work at a very tender age to augment the family income. Out of work-hours there was no other recreation than roaming the roads. I think she was more to be pitied than blamed in that before a wedding ring was placed on her finger she found herself the mother of two children. The world, it is said, offers a two-fold hospitality: a place to be born in, and a place to die in. The sight of my birth-certificate makes me wince when I see the dash where a father's name should be; and when I read the word 'workhouse' yet I tell myself that I should feel something of a sense of gratitude in that somebody received, washed and clothed me and laid

[1]Pickled or soused.

me down to sleep on my first appearance in the world. I dare say the majority of the youngsters in the Union were happy enough, for what one has never had one does not miss. I think the sense of misery that I experience, as I recall it, is due to the fact that there was no sense of security in my little world. A child would become used to large bare rooms and officialdom if it knew nothing else; but if he or she spends a few weeks at a time in a small cottage surrounded by loved relatives and freedom, the bitter contrast at other times was bound to cause a terrible sense of misery and injustice.

How many weeks or months I lived with my grandparents at the cottage before my little world was troubled again I can't say. I was happy, and lived in and for the moment as children will. My happiness was clouded over at times by the ridicule of other children who, because of my cropped head, would call after me, 'old Union maid'. Children can suffer untold humiliation through such things.

I remember once finding some stout clean rope in Grandfather's cupboard, and I got an idea. When nobody was looking I cut a length of this rope and unravelled it. Then standing on a stool before a mirror I tucked the wavy strands up under my long tam-o'-shanter. I then went out of doors and walked struttingly about, flinging the wavy strands over my shoulders in a graceful manner in order to impress other children. Pride goes before a fall, and when half my wavy hair fell out from my tam-o'-shanter on to the ground, the derision of my companions was hard to bear.

Little by little I became aware of the unhappy status of my brother and me. Never shall I forget how the bottom dropped out of my world when in a moment of intense irritation my grandmother said crossly: 'I'm not your Ma. Maud is your Ma.' I just could not take it in at first, but when I knew that she really meant it I broke my heart.

Had our grandmother told us that Susan, or Ann, was our mother it would not have been so bad, for we knew and loved them. But Maud! We hardly knew her, having only seen her a few times in our lives, and then only for what must have been an hour or so. Harry was too young to understand the full significance of what Grandmother had said, but on seeing my distress set up an accompanying howl.

Near our cottage was a hill, at the bottom of which there was an open well in the hedgeway. Many people from the neighbouring village used it for drinking purposes. One sweltering hot summer's day I took Harry by the hand and we both ran down the hill, and, at my suggestion, we both plunged our heads into the well's clear cold waters seeing which of us could hold our breath the longest. Alas for us! We were spotted by some of the villagers, who grabbed and shook us as a dog might shake a rat. 'You bastards! You filthy little bastards!' said more than one angry voice; then we were marched howling to the cottage. The living-room seemed for the next half-hour or so to be filled with a deputation of women all telling my grandparents in the strongest language possible just what ought to be done with those filthy little bastards belonging to their daughter. Indeed, not only was the living-room full but a crowd had gathered outside the door. I do not recall that my grandparents raised their voices, but they must have had a difficult time on our account.

At that early age I did not know the meaning of the word 'bastard'. I only know that the angry tone in which the word was always used conveyed to my sensitive mind the realization that Harry and I were in some dreadful mysterious way different from other children; that indeed we had no right to be in the world at all. It may seem unbelievable to the reader that a child of five or thereabouts could be troubled and weighed down by such thoughts, but such was the case.

Soon after the episode of the well, I very nearly lost the life to which so many people seemed to think I had no right; or perhaps it would be more in accordance with the truth if I say I was very nearly robbed of it.

A party of village children were in the hay-field playing,

when a big hefty boy shouted as he spotted me, "Ere comes that old Union maid; let's roll her in the hay.' I was seized and thrown down upon some hay. Many hands threw more and more hay on top of me, and finally several children jumped on me until every bit of breath was crushed out of my body. I gasped and gasped, and still those youngsters jumped.

I have no recollection of how I was saved, but I think Harry must have run to the cottage and brought someone to the rescue.

One day a tall important-looking stranger spoke to me as I played near the cottage. He asked my age, to which I could give no satisfactory reply. Then he asked where I lived. I pointed to the cottage, and said, 'In there with Ma.'

He must, I think, have been a school inspector, for a day or so later I was taken to the infants' school down the hill, past the fatal well and not far from the Union.

I have good reason to remember that first day at school. The teacher of my class must have been a very thoughtless woman, if not actually cruel. I was called out to the front of the class with two or three other children for talking. 'And now,' said the teacher severely, 'you will stand there until after class and then I shall cut your tongues out.' Never for one moment did I doubt that she meant to carry out her threat. I stood quaking with fear.

The class at length was over and the children trooped out except the biggest child in the class, to whom the teacher said, 'Violet, will you go and ask Miss James to lend me her largest scissors.' My terror at last was overpowering, and I gave one loud piercing scream. The teacher then said, 'Well, I'll let you off this once, but if ever you talk again in school, that tongue will come out.'

I remember with what relief I saw my youngest aunt outside the school, for she had come to fetch me home, and it was not until I was safely in the cottage in my grandmother's arms that I was able to unburden my tears. I remember nothing more of that school.

*   *   *

Once again Harry and I were lying side by side on our little makeshift bed upstairs, when I heard a buzz of conversation in the living-room. Our names were mentioned several times. Sometimes it was Grandmother's voice, sometimes Grandfather's, and sometimes the younger voices of our aunts. I strained every nerve to listen and understand what was being said, for I could tell that the fates of Harry and me were in the balance.

'Well,' said my grandmother, 'if we don't get a letter from Maud during the week, Emma will have to go back to the Union even if Harry doesn't.'

'They'll both have to go,' said Grandfather, then added, 'We can't be expected to take them with us to Plymouth, for even if we could afford to pay their fares, Mrs Roberts won't have room for them. It's very good of her to take us all in as it is, until we can get a home of our own.'

Now it was Auntie Susan who spoke. 'Don't forget, Da, Maudie can't write.'

'I know she can't,' answered Grandfather, 'but Jack O'Brien can – he's a darned good scholar.'

'Well anyhow,' came Auntie Anne's voice, 'I hope them poor kids don't have to go to the Union again, poor little souls.'

'I hope so, too,' said Aunt Susan, then she added: 'Anyhow, if they have to go I'm not taking them. It upsets me to hear the way they both carry on when I've got to leave them, and this time we shan't be here to take them out again.'

'What I can't understand,' said Grandmother, 'is why on earth couldn't Maud have married Cod Murphy seeing he is the father of her children, instead of marrying Jack O'Brien, who won't look at the poor kids; at least he won't have anything to do with Emma, and I very much doubt if he will take Harry.'

'Well,' said Auntie Susan, 'I suppose she would have

married Cod Murphy if somebody hadn't come home from the war and told her lies about Cod being killed.'

'Well, it's a bad job anyway,' said Grandmother, 'and those poor innocent children have got to suffer for other people's wrong-doing.'

The reader may say that a child of five could not possibly have retained a conversation such as I have described above. This was, however, the substance of it, and, as I have said before, it was little by little that I learnt of our unfortunate status. A remark here, and a conversation there, so that years later when recalling that evening I was able to piece the fragments of conversation together to make the sense of it as I have just related.

As I lay there in the darkness with the sleeping Harry by my side, a great fear gripped me. Ma and Da and everybody in my little world were going away, right away, possibly in one of those great big puff-puffs I had heard about and seen for myself going over the bridge at the bottom of the hill, and Harry and I might once again be put into the Union, and this time for ever and ever . . .

Sobs shook me as I cried aloud, waking Harry who started to bellow also. Auntie Susan came upstairs to find out what was the matter. I clung to her, sobbing – 'I – I don't wa – want to go to the U – Union.' 'There, there, lie down and go to sleep like a good girl,' she said kindly, then she added in a determined voice: 'You *shan't* go, not if I can help it.'

Grandmother then came upstairs and soothingly told me I must have been dreaming. By this time Harry was fast asleep again and, to a certain extent comforted and reassured, I followed his example.

The next few days seemed to be all bustle and excitement in our cottage – that is, bustle on our grandmother's part and excitement on the part of my aunts and us two children, for I no longer dreaded the Union, having been assured again and again that Harry and myself were to go to Plymouth with the rest of the household.

Even the fact that we were to be handed over to Maud could not damp our spirits, for were we not going in one of those wonderful puff-puffs? And had we not heard the grown-ups refer to Plymouth as a city with lots of lights and fairs, and there was the sea with its beaches on which Harry and I could play. So long as it was certain we were not going to be put in the Union, the thought of parting from our beloved grandparents did not trouble our heads.

In preparation for the journey Grandmother had a new dress made for me – the one and only new dress I ever had during my childhood. Harry had a new sailor suit. My dress was the colour of crushed strawberry. I heard it described as such – that is how I remember. It arrived from the dressmaker's on the day before the journey. In my excitement I begged to be allowed to put it on just to show other children that I, too, could have a beautiful new dress as well as the best of them.

My poor grandmother gave in at last for the sake of peace and quiet. The moment she put it on, I rushed out of the cottage into the road – and fell headlong into a pool of muddy water. Quite frankly I can't think why I did not after all end up in the Union. Auntie Susan picked me up, and small blame to her that she gave me a good spanking. While I howled she took the dress off, washed it, and ironed it ready for the journey, and not until everybody else was ready the next day was I allowed to have that dress on.

Many people came to see us off the next day, for my grandparents were loved by all their neighbours, and I suppose a railway journey in those days was considered a great adventure. As I was lifted up and placed in the railway carriage, little did I dream what sort of future fate held in store for me.

Had my grandparents known, they would, I am sure, have decided that the Workhouse Union was by far the lesser of the two evils.

CHAPTER 2

Life in a Plymouth Slum

THE DISTANCE BETWEEN REDRUTH AND PLYMOUTH IS SOME sixty miles by rail. The train stopped at every station, and as we came to a standstill each time, one or other of my aunts would thrust her head out of the window, asking anxiously, 'Is this Plymouth?' At last, however, we came to the end of what seemed to us inexperienced travellers an endless journey.

Mrs Roberts, the friend with whom my grandparents and aunts were to stay while they looked for rooms, was at the station to meet us. 'Your daughter Maud has promised to fetch the children this evening,' she said in answer to Grandmother's anxious inquiry.

Tired and sleepy after our journey, Harry and I nevertheless did full justice to a good meal which our kind hostess had prepared for us. Presently there was a knock on the door, and as Mrs Roberts opened it, there stood Maud. She greeted her mother and sisters, and chatted for a while, then rose to take her leave.

'Come, Emma,' she said, 'I'm going to take you to some people I know. Well, my man won't have her home,' she added, as Grandmother started to protest. Grandmother said, 'What about Harry?'

'Well, we're going to keep him,' replied Maud, 'for my

man says a boy may be useful later on when he starts earning, but he won't have Emma,' she said again decidedly.

It was a very sleepy pair of children who were kissed all round by grandparents and aunts, and as Maud led us through the lighted streets I nearly dropped asleep as I walked, or rather dragged myself, along. I was not conscious of caring where I was to sleep.

We came presently to a very poor-looking street. The houses were very tall and shabby-looking. Maud paused before a door and opened it. We went through a long passage and up a dark stairway. A door opened, showing a dim gaslight. A woman stood in the doorway. 'Come in,' she said, as she saw who it was.

'I've brought Emma,' Maud said, as she led me into the room, then added, 'I can't stop; my man will be wondering where I've got to.' Without more ado she left me there among strangers, descending the stairs again, taking Harry with her.

The large tenement room into which Maud had led me was a dirty evil-smelling apartment. Tired and bewildered as I was, I noticed a large cage in one corner of the room in which white rats sported themselves. One was treading on a wheel. The opposite corner contained a rickety-looking bed.

The third corner of the room contained a dirty gas-stove, on the top of which a frying pan was standing from which came a savoury smell of something cooking. Later I learned that only one cooking smell ever pervaded that room – fried bacon scraps and cheese.

The fourth corner contained a heap of dirty rags, old jackets, etc. Very soon I discovered this was to be my sleeping quarters.

A table stood in the centre of the room upon which an oil lamp was now burning instead of the gas jet that had been alight before. Near the table sat a man who might have been about the age of Grandfather, but a greater contrast could hardly be imagined.

The man was bent, had a pointed beard, two fingers missing on his right hand, and his face was evil. His eyes as they fastened themselves on me sent a shudder of fear through me.

Many years later I heard this man described as being like Fagin in *Oliver Twist*; that, I think, was a very apt description.

Mrs Pratt, as I shall call her, was younger than her husband, neither stout nor thin. She was tidy but dirty.

I started to weep and sob as I hung my head, standing there near the rats' cage, for even the interest in these rodents could not keep me from longing for my grandmother and Harry. Mr and Mrs Pratt continued their meal in silence, eating from the same plate.

Presently the woman came over, and as she started to undress me she said roughly, but not unkindly, 'It's no use snivelling, Emma.'

'I – I want my Ma,' was all I could say between my sobs.

'Look, Emma,' the man said, as he rose and came over to me in a threatening manner. 'You belong to us now, so shut yer row and be quiet, do you hear?'

Terrified, I choked back my sobs and allowed myself to be led to the filthy pile of rags in the corner. A dirty jacket was rolled up for my pillow, and as I lay down Mrs Pratt covered me with other dirty jackets and coats. For a while I wept softly, then sleep brought temporary forgetfulness.

I could not have been asleep long before I was awakened by a horrible sense of things crawling over me. I opened my eyes. The lamp was still burning; Mr and Mrs Pratt were reading a newspaper. As realization came upon me of my whereabouts, I turned to face the wall for I could not bear to look upon these people. I was stifled in the filthy bedding; I itched and scratched. Then, to my horror, I saw pink insects creeping up the wall. I put my finger on one to squash it; the smell made me feel sick. I closed my eyes again. I could shut out the sight of those horrid bugs as I later learned to call them, but I could not shut out the smell. I don't think there is a more sickening smell on earth than the smell of bugs, but perhaps I am prejudiced. Turning once again in my efforts to stop the awful itching brought a sharp rebuke from behind the newspaper.

'Lie still and go to sleep, Emma,' Mrs Pratt said severely. I made every effort to obey, then made up my mind I would have a game of pretending. I would pretend that Harry and I were in our own clean little nest in the white-washed cottage at Redruth, and that 'Ma' was only downstairs, through the open bedroom door, and that if I wished I could summon her aid. At length deep sleep, that blessed healer of childish troubles, really did overtake me.

When I awoke I found I was not alone in the filthy shakedown. A boy's head lay on another rolled-up jacket near my own. He was fast asleep with his mouth open. I could do nothing but stare and stare at the strange face. Who was he? And where did he come from? I wondered. It certainly was not Harry. This was a big boy – much, much older than Harry. This phenomenon at least took my mind off bugs and other troubles, for I could think of nothing else as I watched him in silence.

Soon a creaking from the bed told me that the Pratts had awakened. The face to which I had taken such an instinctive dislike the previous evening now presented itself. 'Come on, Charlie,' he shouted, glowering over to our corner. 'Get up, you lazy hound.'

Charlie (for that was the name of my bedmate) made no move, being still fast asleep.

'I won't call you again, you young devil,' said the angry man from the bed. 'Here, take that!' A large hob-nailed boot came hurtling through the air – the cruel heel with its iron caught not Charlie, for whom it was meant, but me, right in the centre of the forehead.

How long it was before I regained consciousness I do

not know, but when I next became aware of things there was
a bandage about my head, which throbbed unmercifully. I felt
sick and ill and did not rise from the sordid shake-down for, I
believe, a couple of days.

The Pratts spoke kindly to me, and poor Charlie, who
I could now see to be a lad of about thirteen or fourteen, was
very good to me, feeling that my suffering was in some way
his fault.

The rats, which were periodically allowed out of the
cage to run about the room, were brought to me one by one,
to make friends with. At first I shrank, but later became
fascinated by the creatures. It took my mind off my troubles
to watch their antics, for they would scamper in and out of
the old coats, getting into pockets and popping up from the
oddest corners. I learned their names and could very soon
tell them apart, odd though it may seem. I would tire quickly
because of the pain in my head; then Charlie would get them
all back into the cage somehow.

I later learned that this poor boy was, like me,
illegitimate, and had been given by his callous mother to Mr
Pratt for purposes which I will record later.

My forehead, which was very badly swollen, continued
to give trouble. No doctor was called in. I think fear, as
well as expense, was the reason for this; but Mr Pratt had
some knowledge of herbs – he and Charlie used to go out
into the country and on their return they would open dirty
handkerchiefs in which they had put leaves they had freshly
gathered. They were round, sappy kind of leaves; they called
them 'penny-cakes'. Whether that is the correct name for
them or not I have never been able to find out, for on the
rare occasions that I have seen the leaves growing in hedges,
not one single person that I have asked has ever been able
to name them. These leaves were placed in large quantities
on the bump on my forehead, then kept in place by a rag for
bandage. The leaves did their work, for one day blessed relief
came. The bump burst – a whole lot of pus and matter came

away, after which healing took place. Everyone who saw me predicted that I would carry the scar all my life, and they were right. I have something with which to remember Mr Pratt every time I look in a mirror. (Not that I could ever forget the monster.)

One day soon after these events, Mrs Pratt called me over to the window. I joined her, a rat on each shoulder. She pointed across the street, just as the notes of a barrel organ, or hurdy-gurdy as we called it, came floating up to us. 'Look,' she said, 'there's Da and Charlie.' 'Da' was Mr Pratt, who had insisted upon my addressing him in this manner as I was to pass for his own daughter. Mr Pratt was playing the organ; a crowd of children, mostly girls, were dancing to the tunes. I had never seen anything like it before, and watched fascinated as the girls danced with utter abandon, twirling their legs round and round, first the right leg then the left, each time tapping the toes on the ground then flinging the leg right up in the air. I urged that I, too, might be allowed out in the street and try to perform this wonderful dance.

'Oh no you don't,' she said, 'or we shall have the school inspector here. We're going travelling soon, so it's no use your starting school here.'

I did not bother to question her as to what she meant by travelling, for I was too interested in the scene below. The tune had changed now, so had the dance. Windows had been thrown up, and tenants were leaning out resting their chins on their hands as they listened and watched. Coppers were thrown down from windows and passers-by.

Charlie was picking them up and placing them in his cap. He looked up and waved to me. As he did so, Mrs Pratt pulled me away from the window. 'I don't want you to be seen too much,' she said, 'specially when your forehead is sore. Now mind, if anybody asks how you got that scar, you tell them you fell down.'

'Yes, Ma,' I said meekly, as a rat dived under the collar of my dress and scampered down my leg on to the floor, then dashed to its cage and started the wheel turning madly. Whether the scene below had excited it or not, I cannot say.

My new crushed strawberry dress that my dear grandmother had had made for me, and which fitted me so well, had been replaced by a ragged dress that had been purchased at a nearby second-hand dealer's for a couple of pence. I never saw my new dress again. The only washing I ever had was a smear with a flannel over face and hands; my hair was never brushed and hardly ever combed. Our meals were always the same; whatever time of the day Mrs Pratt decided to cook, scraps of cheese and bacon was the menu.

When my forehead was healed I was allowed to go out to the nearest grocer's after school hours, when there was no danger of my being noticed by an inspector. Always the errand was the same: 'Please for two-penn'orth of cheese and bacon bits,' I would ask. The bits would be put aside for me as before they had been kept for Charlie.

The method of cooking was this: first Mrs Pratt fried the bits of bacon, then the bits of cheese. Then while the cheese was still in the pan, a little water was poured in and boiled up; a little pepper was added, and there was the meal. This liquid was then placed in one's dish, and bread would be soaked in it. I never remember any other diet all the time I lived with the Pratts. Mr and Mrs Pratt always shared a soup plate between them, and it was an odd sight to see first one and then the other dip their bread in.

Charlie and I used saucers; one each, I'm glad to say.

No washing was ever performed in this family. Underclothing was worn until dropping to pieces, when it was replaced with another garment bought at the aforesaid second-hand dealer's for a penny or so.

I had been with the Pratts for perhaps two or three weeks, during which time I was learning to get accustomed to my new existence and to being without my grandparents and

Harry (though there were still times when the longing for the little white-washed cottage and all that I had called home was hard to bear) when one evening I found myself alone with Mr Pratt. For a while he sat looking at me in an evil way that made me afraid. At last he said, 'Come here, Emma.' I obeyed, slowly. This beast – old enough to be my grandfather – grabbed hold of me, a child about six years of age, if I was that. He undid some of my clothing and behaved in a disgusting way. Presently he said, 'Don't tell Ma or Charlie what I've done, or something awful will happen.' As he said this his face was so evil and threatening that I was overwhelmed with fear.

The reader might well ask what of my grandparents all this time – did they make no move at all to see that I was in safe hands? I can only reply by reminding the reader that, though they were living in the same town, they had their own problems, having to look for a settled home. My grandfather, as the reader will remember, was a blind man. My grandmother's own sight was fast failing, and she was in poor health. My aunts had to get settled in work, and in any case I very much doubt if at that time they had been informed of my address by my irresponsible mother.

Then again, though through such splendid men as Dr Barnardo and General Booth and others of their like much had already been done for the child of the underworld, there were still far too many waifs and strays whom no such organization had touched. And anyhow, in those days, the average illegitimate child was considered of very little importance. Maud did not come either.

There was constant bickering between Charlie and Mr Pratt. The poor boy could do nothing right. Very soon I learned that he had been handed over when about the same age as I then was. The poor ragged child had been used to attract pity, just in the same way as I was to be used shortly. For I soon found that the Pratts were wanderers, periodically tramping from place to place between the town of Plymouth and Penzance in Cornwall.

21

Sometimes on these excursions a barrel organ was hired and used to get money. Sometimes they sang Sankey and Moody's hymns which had an appeal that touched the pockets of kind-hearted listeners. The reader will appreciate that the sight of a ragged child would touch the heart of a potential giver much more readily than the sight of two unaccompanied adults.

Now, however, Charlie had outgrown this stage. People were always saying that a great hulking lad such as he should be working. The boy was willing to work, but up to the present had not been allowed to seek it. Now, however, I was to take his place – that is, as soon as the Pratts started travelling. Charlie was constantly being told he could go to the Devil.

The lad had earned a few odd coppers at times by breeding the white rats which he sold to other boys for sixpence each. It was to him a fascinating hobby, which brought interest into his life as well as profit.

The reader will shrink with horror at the thought of a cage of rats in a room where people ate and slept. So should I now, but at that time I shared Charlie's interest in the creatures; the smell, which would now offend my nostrils, became part of the general atmosphere of the room, and one grew accustomed to it.

Now Jennie, the mother rat, was to have a new brood, and Charlie was going to turn the last family into cash. The boy confided to me that night in a whisper that he was saving up his pence unknown to Pratt and that he intended at the first opportunity to run away. Though Charlie was several years older than myself, we had the common bond of our misfortunes between us, and the lad talked to me more, I suppose, than would be the case if we were indeed brother and sister in a happy household.

'Where will you go, Charlie?' I asked anxiously, for I knew vaguely that if people had no home at all they would probably starve. Also I was dismayed on my own account, for we had been friends since the kind-hearted boy had realized that I had suffered on his account, when the iron heel of the boot Pratt had so cruelly thrown at him had caught my forehead by mistake.

'I shall tramp to Penzance by degrees,' the boy replied. 'I've had to do it many times before, and when I get to Penzance I know somebody that will take me in because she said she would.'

Thus satisfied on his account, though still anxious on my own, I snuggled close to this, my only friend, and we both fell asleep.

CHAPTER 3

The Hurdy-Gurdy Man

HOW LONG I HAD BEEN WITH THE PRATTS WHEN WE SET OUT
one morning on the first stage of our journey to Penzance I
cannot say; probably a few weeks.

Charlie, true to his word, had run away. Even I did not
know just when he was going. One day he was there, the
next he was missing. I do not remember that Pratt or his wife
discussed the matter. Probably they had known all along that
the boy would run away in time, and as he had outgrown his
usefulness they took no steps to retrieve him. Almost at once
they announced the fact that we were starting for Saltash, a
little town about four or five miles away where we were to put
up for the night.

The fact that we were leaving the town behind that
contained my grandparents and Harry did not worry me
greatly, for was I not going back to Cornwall? And as the
Pratts had assured me that we should indeed pass through
the town of Redruth itself on the way to Penzance, I was
greatly excited; though I knew that Grandmother was now
living in Plymouth and therefore could not be in the cottage
at Redruth Church town, yet somehow in a vague sort of way
I expected to find things as they were.

Pratt had bought or hired a donkey to pull the hurdy-
gurdy, now that Charlie was no longer available for the

purpose. When I grew too tired to walk, I would ride on the shafts in front of the organ, much to poor Neddy's disgust, for I was a heavy child. I loved that donkey at once, and have ever since had a weakness for the species, though it is years now since I beheld one.

Every now and then we came to a standstill before some house or farm or cottage with gardens gay with flowers. Mr and Mrs Pratt took it in turns to turn the handle of the organ, and I would run and pick up pennies that dropped from windows. Sometimes a young mother would come to the door clutching a small boy who reminded me of Harry. At such times I would catch my breath and want to cry.

Looking back, it seems to me that these cottagers were wonderfully kind to me. Sometimes a kindly mother would say: 'Wait a minute, I'll get you a glass of milk, dear, and could you eat a piece of cake?' to which I always replied in the affirmative. Children were a mixed lot; some would point to me saying: 'Look, Ma, see that poor little girl?' Other nicely dressed children would stare at me with a look of disdain.

Thus in time we arrived in Saltash where the Pratts made a bee-line for a common lodging house where they were well known. The landlady expressed no surprise when she saw me. I think Charlie had probably stayed there recently and told her about me. The only luggage we had with us had been placed in the box built between the donkey shafts and the organ. The donkey had been fed and put into a stable for the night. The organ was put under cover; the inevitable frying-pan, bread, cheese and bacon, brought out of the shaft-box, and Mrs Pratt proceeded to cook the evening meal on the common stove where men lodgers were also cooking, or so I think.

I cannot describe these lodging houses (for in due course I slept in several). I can only recall the invariable kindliness shown towards me. Always I was the only child lodger, though occasionally I met children of the various landladies.

The only thing beside kindliness I can remember are

comforting fireplaces from which various cooking smells all mixed up emerged; added to this the haze and smell of tobacco smoke. Yes, one other thing I remember is that a large percentage of the wayfarers were Italian. It amused me to watch foreign gestures, which I would imitate. I would also make gabbling sounds at the same time and really believed I was speaking Italian, or as we called it, 'Eyetalyan'.

After our meal of cheese and bacon that evening in the lodging house at Saltash, I sat passively resting for a while watching the other lodgers and listening to the different voices, when the landlady suggested I'd better go off to bed. The good woman preceded Mrs Pratt and me with a lighted candle and showed us into a bedroom which, accustomed as I had been to the filthy tenement apartment in Plymouth, seemed to me a palace.

Mrs Pratt turned back the bedclothing from the bottom of the bed. 'Get in here,' she said, after taking off my things, 'and lie across the foot of the bed.'

I went to sleep almost at once, for I had been on the road for several hours, and though the bed was certainly not free from fleas, bugs there were none. Moreover, the blankets felt good after the dirty jackets, etc., to which I had grown accustomed.

I awakened a few hours later to feel two nasty pairs of feet pressing into me on the one side, and the cold iron bedstead pressing up against me on the other; for Mr and Mrs Pratt had come to bed, and as they pressed their feet against me they also pulled up the bedding. To make matters worse I was scolded if I moved. Needless to say, sleep was much disturbed. I had to grow accustomed to this method of sleeping, however, for that is how I always had to lie when in lodging houses.

One word about these common lodging houses in which we stayed.

I have an idea, though it is only vague, that the bed in

which the Pratts slept and which I shared, was not always the only bed in the room. I cannot really be certain of this, however, and therefore will not make any definite statement one way or another. If it seems odd that my memory should let me down on such an important point, the reader must remember that always on these occasions I was dead tired after a heavy day's tramp. Moreover, one good thing can be said in Mrs Pratt's favour: she did send me early to bed when possible, so that other lodgers could have slept in the room and left again without my knowledge.

We continued in this manner for the rest of the journey to Penzance. I would walk or ride behind Neddy on the donkey shafts. We would stop now and then, play the organ and collect coins, until finally we reached the town for which we were making, and again we would put up at the lodging house to which the Pratts had come on the previous visit. My stockings became more and more holey, making walking difficult. Some things I enjoyed – the buzz of telegraph poles, the song of birds, the gay flowers in cottage gardens – and though I suppose now there would be much I should shrink from in a common lodging house, as a child I found it all interesting. As I have said before, there was much kindliness among our fellow wayfarers. Then, again, more than once I have known some kindly landlady supply me with a decent pair of her own child's stockings, which for a time at least made life more bearable.

It may have taken us ten days or a fortnight to reach Penzance in this manner, one or two days having to be spent at our lodgings on account of bad weather.

The day before we arrived at our destination we passed through my native town of Redruth, and to my bitter disappointment we did not touch Church town; so that, after all, I did not see our beloved little whitewashed cottage or any dear familiar face. I did not realize then, as I did later, that this was arranged on purpose so that I should not be recognized. It was dusk as we drew near to

Penzance. We could see the lamp-lighter busy along the quay front.

It was a very tired little girl that rode on the donkey shafts. It was difficult not to fall asleep to the rhythm of the animal's footsteps in the silence of the evening. We stopped at our destination, a lodging house in a side street. As we entered the house a babel of Italian voices greeted us. The landlord himself was of this nationality, which may have accounted for the popularity his house had among his fellow countrymen. We were led through a shed, from which emerged the savoury smell of hot baked potatoes. We saw a potato oven on wheels, which the landlord explained he was just going to pull up the street, where in the chill of the evening he would have a quick sale. As he handed us over to the care of his daughter, he opened his oven door and, taking out a red-hot potato, placed it in my hands, telling me in broken English to put it into my 'pinny' so as not to burn myself. To a tired, hungry child that potato was a feast of the gods, and made an excellent change from the usual diet of cheese and bacon.

We were shown to an outside loft which was to be our home while in Penzance – a sort of ladder stairway had to be ascended to get to it. The loft was whitewashed and fairly-clean. It contained an iron bedstead, a small deal table, and two Windsor chairs.

I cannot remember what the cooking arrangements were, but somehow the cheese and bacon meals did appear. Mr Pratt joined us after feeding and bedding Neddy for the night and putting up the hurdy-gurdy.

There was another of these organs in the shed, and we soon found it belonged to an Italian, who boasted a monkey as well. This little creature fascinated me. It wore a red jacket and a tiny red cap. When out with its master it used to hold out a cap for coins as the organ played. People were fond of giving the monkey chip-potatoes, and what the creature managed to put away was amazing.

Our organ had a green baize cover which protected the woodwork. This was now removed, and Pratt brought it up to the loft, for it to be placed on the floor. This was to be my bed. Well, anyhow, it was better than being pressed between two pairs of unsavoury feet and the bars of a cold iron bedstead.

The first day at Penzance we did not take Neddy and the organ out. Mr Pratt took me for a long walk to the neighbouring fishing village of Newlyn. The man had brought a bag, for well he knew that if he hung about the boats long enough, as they were being unloaded, some fine mackerel would be given him by kind-hearted fishermen. His expectations were justified, for presently a big burly fellow with a rich Cornish accent shouted to me: 'Here, my dear, want these for dinner, do 'ee?' As he spoke he picked up four large, gleaming mackerel and handed them to me.

I was standing perilously near the edge of the quay, and some of the seagulls which had been screaming overhead now swooped down so near to my face that in my fright I let the fish fall into the water. 'Don't cry, little maid,' said the kind-hearted man as my pinafore went up to my eyes. 'Here's four more for 'ee.' This time I grabbed the mackerel tight and walked triumphantly towards Mr Pratt, who in the meantime had started to sing for coppers which were readily forthcoming from the boats. Whether or not the seagulls were alarmed at Mr Pratt's voice I can't say, but they left me in peace.

Pratt took the fish and placed it in the bag he had brought for the purpose, then collected the last coin that had been thrown on the slippery quayside, and we wended our way homewards to Penzance and the loft.

Those mackerel tasted good when fried. I have written earlier on that I could not recall ever having anything but cheese and bacon while living with the Pratts. It was only as I recalled the memory of that fishing village that our one alternative diet presented itself to my mind, for when living at Penzance it was always possible to go to Newlyn quay and bring home a bagful of fresh fish without paying one penny for the privilege.

On the way home Pratt said: 'I'm going to take you to Newlyn with the hurdy-gurdy tomorrow. "Ma" will stay at home.'

The next day we set out with Neddy and the organ. We stopped once or twice before we reached Newlyn. We passed at least two organs on the way. One of these was the organ I had seen in the shed, standing beside our own. The monkey was alternately springing up on his master's shoulder, then to the top of the organ, its wicked little eyes surveying the crowd of youngsters who had gathered round, for it was Saturday and consequently a school holiday. I begged Pratt to wait for a few minutes while we watched the little fellow in his bright red coat and hat. Seeing a couple of adults make a halt and put their hands to their pockets, the monkey excitedly took his master's cap (which the man had held out to him with one hand while he turned the handle with the other) and with a comical pleading expression held it up for the coins which were laughingly placed in it.

Pratt was impatient. 'Come on,' he said, 'or that fellow will get to Newlyn before us, and we shan't do very well.' I still lingered, gazing at the interesting spectacle of the monkey, now eating chip-potatoes out of a paper bag which some passer-by had given it. Pratt lifted me on to the donkey shaft without more ado, and Neddy set off at a brisk trot.

We halted before a little row of shops. Pratt helped me down from the shaft. 'You must collect the money now, Emma,' he said. The inevitable crowd of children gathered as the organ's tinny notes came over the air. 'Goodbye, Dolly, I must leave you' appeared to be a favourite tune, judging by the way the audience supplied the words. Then came 'The Boers have got my Daddy, my soldier Dad'; as children bawled lustily, one or two white-aproned women standing in doorways wiped their eyes. Now the patriotic songs of the day gave way to the more cheerful notes of 'Chase me, Charlie', when instantly the girls in the crowd started to do the corkscrew dance that had so intrigued me when I first beheld it in Plymouth. Pratt handed me his cap, as I had seen the other organ-grinder do to his monkey, and like the monkey I tried to put on a pathetic look as I held it up to the passer-by. Soon pennies rained from upper windows as well as from open doorways. Occasionally a well-dressed girl would come towards me gracefully, and having tossed her beautiful tresses over her shoulder, would place a coin in the cap with the air of a princess.

I gathered up the coins from the pavement and gutter, and as I handed them to Pratt a woman came out of a little general dealer's shop with something in her hand. Coming over to me she said tenderly as she thrust a paper bag into my hand, 'Here, my dear, here's some Kruger's Whiskers for you.' I took the bag eagerly as I thanked the giver. How could she have known, I wondered, that Kruger's Whiskers were the one thing I desired most at that moment, having a few minutes before caught sight of them in the window, displayed between Spanish shoe-laces and bags of sherbet? Kruger's Whiskers, I must explain to the reader, were little shreds of cocoa-nut sweetened and coloured brown with chocolate. Harry and I had on rare occasions had this delectable sweetmeat when at home with Grandmother. It was a great favourite with us. While Pratt was counting and putting away the coppers, I generously gave Neddy a share of the Whiskers. Clutching hold of the donkey's neck affectionately, I asked if he had ever in all his life tasted such lovely Whiskers. Neddy shook his head vigorously. It may, of course, have been the flies that were bothering his ears – a grown-up would certainly have said so. On my questioning him solemnly whether he would like another bit he brayed loudly. 'You *shall*,' I said, dividing the last few Whiskers with him.

We now set off again for another part of the village and came to a halt before a row of fishermen's cottages. The gardens were very picturesque and in full bloom with red geraniums, fuchsias (how I loved those droopy fuchsias!), marigolds, and every sort of flower one could desire. After Pratt had played through the usual set of tunes and I had gathered the coins, one fisherman's wife asked me if I would like a bunch of flowers, as she had noticed me looking at them longingly. With the delight of a child, I accepted. The kind-hearted soul gathered me a lovely bouquet, blending the colours together as tastefully as if it were for a queen. I buried my nose in the rich perfume, then asked my friend Neddy to smell. This time Neddy was not interested.

After a couple more stops Pratt said, 'We will go along this road and turn in at the next gate and eat our bread and cheese in the field.'

When we reached the field he took the donkey out of the shafts and let him graze. Then leaving me for a few minutes he climbed over a gate into the next field and came back with a swede turnip. Sitting beside me on a bank he got out his penknife and peeled the turnip, then offered me a slice. Thus we sat eating bread, cheese, and raw turnip.

This was the first time I had been really alone with Pratt since that one evening in the tenement room in Plymouth of which I have told in a previous page. Again I was conscious of a shrinking fear as once more he looked at me as he did on that occasion. My fears were justified for once again I became the victim of this old man's desire. He did not actually hurt me physically, but he did as on the former occasion interfere with me in an indecent manner. Again there were veiled threats as to what would happen if I told, and needless to say, wild horses could not have dragged it out of me.

Somehow, in some vague sort of way, the lovely summer's day was spoiled. Even my bunch of flowers seemed to have lost some of their scent and beauty.

Pratt did not drink or visit public houses except for the purpose of collecting coins after playing the organ. I do not remember that he used much bad language, or obscene talk, but he was quite unfit to be in charge of a young child.

I have just said that Pratt did not drink. This was true, but from scraps of conversation to which I listened I gathered that it had not always been so. In his young days he had been in the Merchant Navy and at that time was a heavy drinker. Moreover, I was led to believe that the loss of the two fingers on his right hand had some connexion with this.

The man rose and harnessed the donkey. 'We'll make one more stop,' he said, 'and then we'll make for home.'

When we arrived back in the loft, I believe Mrs Pratt had her suspicions, for her jaw was set and she looked grimmer than usual. However, she did not question me, and after the evening meal I rolled myself up in the green organ cover, and for a while at least my mind was at rest as, in common with children of all states of life, I entered the magic world of dreams.

CHAPTER 4

Fairs and Fairgrounds

IF I HAD ANY SCHOOLING AT THIS STAGE I DO NOT REMEMBER it. All I can recall are frequent visits to the neighbouring villages. Pratt would always take me, but Mrs Pratt would stay at home in the loft or occasionally hire herself out to a hand-laundry for a few hours. That I ever had a clean pinafore at all for my frequent journeys must have been due to these visits to the laundry, for the woman never did any washing at home, and the rest of my clothing would drop to pieces upon me until replaced by some gift from a kindhearted woman who had children of her own and who pitied my condition. Particularly did I suffer from sticky ragged stockings which were never washed or mended. I would have to pull the toes down under the foot further and further in my efforts to get some covering for my heels, which all the time I was with the Pratts suffered from a succession of blisters. To this day I can still in imagination feel those sticky bumps under my feet. As a matter of routine my blisters were pricked nightly, and strange to relate I do not remember that they ever became septic.

I have said I do not remember any schooling at this stage. An exception must be made in favour of Sunday School, for odd though it may seem, the Pratts encouraged my attendance at the little Methodist chapel quite near. Mrs

Pratt would make me a little more presentable than usual; not much, however, for other children of the district, poor as most of them were, usually gave me a wide berth on the Chapel seat. Judging by all that happened later, I have always suspected that I was sent to Sunday School so that I should learn and retain by heart the familiar Sankey and Moody hymns which in the future I was to sing in the streets. Be that as it may, the Sunday School became the brightest thing in my existence, and I eagerly drank in the story of the Saviour's love for children. As if to make up for my being shunned by the other pupils, the teacher always seemed to make a special point of being kind to me.

Mrs Pratt for the most part was utterly indifferent to me. She fed me, and once a day wiped over my face and hands with a flannel. But there her duties ended, except for pricking blisters. Once only do I remember her looking at me with kindly interest, and then she said, 'I had a little maid once, Emma. She would be nearly grown up now.' Then she added, as if talking to a grown-up, 'That was before I married "Da".' 'Where is she?' I asked. 'The vicar in my home adopted her,' she replied simply. Then her face set in its usual indifferent look, and I was afraid to question her further. She never mentioned the subject again.

I am not certain as to what age I was at this time, but I think I was probably between six and seven. I was big, and fortunately pretty strong, for my age.

On our journeys to nearby villages I particularly liked calling at farms, except for one or two where turkeys would come gobbling at me; of these I was terrified. Not only were we pretty sure to do well in the matter of coins, sometimes even a shilling coming our way, but always I could be certain of a glass of skimmed milk, of which I was particularly fond, plus a good slice of that particular brand of home-made cake for which Cornwall was noted.

One day when we were in the little village of St Just, a woman who had noticed me walking lame while collecting money asked Pratt if I could come into her cottage and sit down while she tried a pair of her little girl's boots on to me. Pratt gladly assented, and for a while let Neddy graze by the roadside while he sat down to smoke his pipe. The woman seated me on a polished Windsor chair that reminded me of Grandmother's, it was so clean and bright, as indeed was the rest of the furniture in the room. As my benefactor went upstairs to find the promised footwear, my eyes took in the details of the little parlour. Not only were the chairs like those in the dear white-washed cottage at Redruth, but there on the wall was the very same picture of Queen Victoria, and – yes – there, too, was Daniel in the lions' den. Only Moses was missing. I almost expected to see the two horses with the riders as I looked at the mantelpiece, but this time it was a pair of china dogs that met my eye. In one corner, sure enough, stood a grandfather clock, though not quite so handsome as the one at home in Redruth. The homeliness of it all made me want to cry, so great was the longing for 'Ma' (as I still thought of Grandmother) and all that with which I associated her. I must have begun to cry, for when the kind woman came downstairs with the boots she said concernedly, 'What's the matter, my dear? Don't you want some nice boots?' 'Yes, please,' I said, choking back the tears. How could I have explained what was the matter?

I don't think any boots that came my way were ever the right size; either they seemed too small and hurt that way, or else they were too large and rubbed my heels. In this case it was the latter fault. They were, however, whole and not burst at the sides like the ones I had just left off, and, oh joy! the kind woman had brought me a clean darned pair of stockings as well. How good those stockings felt on me nobody could appreciate unless they had been in similar circumstances. My new friend turned up her nose as she removed my ragged and dirty stockings. 'I'll burn them,' she said.

I felt very comfortable and proud as I put my feet to the ground. I hope I looked as grateful as I felt.

The next stop was in the main street, and the usual crowd of children stood round as the organ played. As the tune 'The Boers have got my Daddy' was being played, one small boy stood and manfully accompanied it with the words which he had evidently been taught very carefully. His little hands were moving to illustrate the words.

> 'The Boers have got my Daddy,
> My soldier Dad.
> I don't like to hear my Mammy sigh
> I don't like to see my Mammy cry,
> I'm going in a big ship, across the ocean wave,
> I'm going out to fight the Boers, I am
> And bring my Daddy home again.'

His chest stuck out manfully as he clenched his fists like a prize fighter about to spring.

Our organ, as I should have mentioned before, had at the top in front a revolving picture. I do not remember if there was more than one picture; I do remember that one, however. It was a brightly coloured picture of the 'Last Supper', though I did not know at the time what it was. It used to interest children very much. I do not suppose they wondered any more than I did why an organ that played the tunes of songs should display sacred pictures.

The group of children, including the curly-headed youngster who had sung the song, suddenly dispersed, shouting gleefully. The reason for this desertion was soon evident, for there, coming towards us, was our fellow lodger – the other organ-grinder – and there, perched on his master's shoulder scratching his leg, was Bruce the monkey in his little red jacket and cap.

As the organ passed us the two men nodded curtly, and Bruce looked back, making a rude gesture with his thumb to his nose. I believe his master taught him to do that to other organs.

*   *   *

Just how long we lived at Penzance that first time I cannot say. Of the first winter spent with Mr and Mrs Pratt I have no recollection whatever. I know that some time or other we made the return journey to Plymouth. I do not think it could have been in the same year,[1] for when next we settled in Plymouth I was certainly older. I remember vaguely that we stayed at the same lodging houses, and that I met the same kindly treatment from the various landladies. I remember dimly, too, my being disappointed again as we passed through Redruth that we did not go near Church town; so that I did not get one glimpse of our dear cottage and the tree with its stone seat round it where Harry and I used to play.

When we settled again in Plymouth we lived in the same poor street on the same side, and if it was not the same tenement room that we had lived in before, it was very like it. The day after we had settled in, great was my excitement when, opening the door in response to a knock, there stood my beloved grandfather and Aunt Susan who had led him here. I hugged him so tight that the poor man begged for mercy. Just as in the old days – 'Let me feel how much you've grown,' he said. I stood on a chair – or box, I forget which – and thinking I could persuade him to believe I had grown all that much, I lifted his hand to the top of my head. Grandfather could pretend as well as me, so he expressed his delight that I was now as tall as he was.

Then he told me that he and Grandma had come to live a few doors away. I gathered by his way of speaking that the move to Plymouth had not been such a beneficial one after all, for they had to move more than once, each time to a cheaper home, until here they were in this dingy street. Mrs Pratt grudgingly allowed me to go with Grandfather in to see my dear grandmother. Oh, how changed I found her! She

---

[1] I have since worked this out and now know that we returned the same year.

could hardly see me, her sight had so failed, and even to my young eyes she looked ill. Grandfather, being blind already, was spared the sight of the change in his wife.

I hugged her as if I could never let her go again. I remember she was (in spite of her failing sight) peeling apples.

My Aunt Susan was now married, so was Auntie Anne who lived some distance away and did not often see her parents. Mr and Mrs Pratt did not encourage visits, so although my grandparents now lived so near I seldom saw them.

This time there was no rats' cage in the tenement room. The only difference I could see was in the two or three fly-blown pictures on the walls. One of these, I remember, was of a shipwreck, and the agonized faces struggling in the water used to make me feel queer if I looked too long at it. The other was of a soldier falling in battle while his comrades appeared to be all lying lifeless around him. Horses with strained appearance were charging into the thick of it all.

My bed, as before, was a makeshift arrangement on the floor, and as before bugs infested walls and bedding.

There may have been at least one chair, but for the most part we sat on orange boxes. The greasy, dusty mantelshelf contained two large vases, both chipped at the top, and so coated with greasy dirt that one could never see the real pattern through; a box of matches, some paper spills, and a few bits of twine here and there were the only ornaments.

In cold weather a little fire burnt in the grate. Though Pratt sometimes fetched the coal for this in small quantities from a nearby dealer's, it was not unusual for me to be sent for two- or three-pennyworth, which I would carry in a sack over my shoulder.

Fruit we got plentiful and cheap from a fruiterer's not far away; not whole fresh fruit certainly, but still fruit, sweet and juicy. The way to get it was this: Mrs Pratt would give me a penny and send me down with her basket, and I would have to say, 'Please can I have a penn'orth of rotten oranges?' The basket would be filled with the rotten oranges for which I had asked, and rotten anything else that happened to be around. Much of what I bought with the penny had to be thrown in the yard dustbin, but the parts that could be eaten were, as I have stated, sweet and juicy. As I write, memories long since forgotten come back to me. I must correct the earlier statement that cheese and bacon was the only diet, for I remember that when we were living at Plymouth, Pratt would sometimes go to the beach and come home with his large, dirty red handkerchief filled with limpets. These Mrs Pratt would boil and we ate them with vinegar. I don't think she could have cooked them properly though, for they always tasted of sand and grit.

Sometimes I was sent with Pratt to pick these limpets off the rocks. I believe when we got a good many they sold them to cooked-meat shops. Now that I was older, it was my duty to fetch up the can of water each day from the yard below. The can was much too heavy for me when filled, and I never managed to get upstairs to our tenement room without slopping the water all over the stairs. The stairs were bare and uncarpeted, however, so that it did not matter much.

Sometimes when sent on an errand I visited my grandparents, though I knew Mrs Pratt did not approve of this, and therefore my visits were few and far between for fear of being found out. I remember about this time, on one such visit, listening intently to a neighbour reading a newspaper aloud to my grandfather. This brought back memories of the cottage at Redruth once again, where I had so often sat quietly listening while one or other of our friendly neighbours would do the same. Always they were men, and though I cannot recall the features of any of these men, how well I remember Grandfather's intelligent look as he would turn his sightless eyes in the reader's direction, and interrupt him with a question or some comment. Odd, I suppose, that a small child could find pleasure in such things, but so it was.

Well, on this occasion there seemed a general air of sadness everywhere, and the reading matter was all about the death of Queen Victoria. To me she was just a lady in the picture, but I loved her, because she *was* in the picture and was one of my first memories, belonging as she did to that dear cottage that now seemed so far away. The picture had not been brought to Plymouth I think, for I have no recollection of it there. In fact the only thing I can be sure of that my grandparents still possessed of the old home was the mahogany chest-of-drawers with the chandeliers on top, already mentioned, and which, as I have stated, is now in the possession of my mother.

Queen Victoria, the lady of the picture, was dead, and everybody was sorry. That is as far as my memory will take me about that.

I can now definitely fix my age, for the good Queen passed away just before my seventh birthday. I did not know at that time when my birthday was, or what my correct age. Always my age was in my mind connected in some way with the departure for Australia of my Uncle Fred, the one son whom my grandmother had managed to rear, for I well remember when any visitor to the cottage asked in my hearing what my age was, the same reply would be forthcoming: 'Well, now, let me see – my boy went to Australia when she was a baby in the cradle, for I know the last thing he ever did was to take her up and kiss her.' Then would follow a lengthy discussion as to what else took place at the same time, and I presume that by this means the visitor's curiosity was satisfied. I was, as already stated, big and strong for my age, and it was not until nearing my twelfth birthday that I knew for certain how old I was. This knowledge then came about because Pratt said he was certain I was about fourteen, and he wished me to leave school altogether so that I could be with him always on his expeditions. The school authorities demanded a birth certificate, when it was finally proved that I was twelve the following January.

It must have been, then, about my seventh birthday that I started to go to school for the second time, for the reader will remember that I did go once at least at Redruth.

The first day at my new school leaves a nasty impression on my mind, though not so dreadful as the other memory. Mrs Pratt had asked the daughter of one of the tenants in the building to take me to her school a few streets away. I have a confused memory of a very large building and what seemed hundreds of children, and I felt very unhappy because I did not know what all the lessons and things were about. In fact I felt odd and out of place, besides being oppressed with an awful shut-in, imprisoned feeling.

The miserable climax came after school, when being buffeted about by boisterous, excited youngsters in a hurry to get on their hats and jackets to get home I found myself outside on the pavement crying my eyes out because I was 'lost'; the girl who had promised to bring me home having apparently forgotten all about me. Every boy and girl had gone, and there was I alone and the street was deserted. At last a woman came by, and seeing the distress I was in asked what was the matter. 'I'm lost,' was all I could say between my sobs. She then asked what street I lived in, and when I said, 'K-K-King Street,' the kind soul said, 'Well, don't cry, you're not far away. Come on, I'll take you.' I dried my eyes and, clutching hold of her hand, soon found myself in familiar surroundings. And that is the only thing I can remember about *that* school, though I think I continued to go by fits and starts for a while.

Fits and starts it was, for when Pratt decided to take out the organ I had to go with him. The fair had come to Plymouth; Pratt had an engagement to play his hurdy-gurdy on the stage outside the lions' cages. I went with him, but only as a spectator, for there were no coppers to be picked up as he was to be paid for his services by Mr Hancock, the owner of the menagerie. I was given a free pass to go in behind the scenes to see the lions; this was a great treat.

A stage was erected before the lions' house, and several girls all dressed in bright picturesque dresses and headgear danced to the tunes of the organ. The scene to me was breath-taking – talk about the corkscrew dance! I had never beheld it done like this before. I thought that nothing could be so wonderful on earth as to be dressed like that, and to be able to throw one's legs in the air, showing wonderful lacy garments beneath the dresses.

The fairground was full of Italians, many of whom I had met before in lodging-houses or on the road; and there, too, was our old friend Bruce in a bright new jacket and cap. The monkey was doing what I had so often seen him do at Penzance – eating chip-potatoes. Italian women all contributed to the brightness of the scene with their bright-coloured head scarves.

Somebody took me in to see the lions, which so excited me I could not sleep that night – so magnificent, so utterly wonderful did they seem to me.

Cheap-jacks were crying their wares. One medical quack was shouting something about his pills. 'Ladies and gentlemen,' he said, 'one lady told me that before taking my pills she weighed twenty stone. A week after taking the pills she could crawl through a sausage without disturbing the meat.'

The Italians were selling baked potatoes from ovens with a cheerful fire beneath. Some were selling chips; some 'Hokey pokey, penny a lump,' adding, 'That's the stuff to make you jump!' Hokey pokey was, if I remember, a sort of hard icecream.

Then there was the penny gaff.[1] Somehow I got into that, but it frightened me and I did not enjoy it. There was too much bang-bang, shoot-shoot about it.

The second evening of the fair, Pratt got me a free pass to 'the living pictures'. Cinema-goers will smile at this

---

[1]Low-class theatre.

43

description, but that is the name by which we called it. Compared with present-day movies I suppose it would seem very primitive, but to me that night it was a foretaste of fairyland. What fun the pillow fights were, with their showers and showers of feathers! Then, too, I remember the man on stilts. What a wonderful sight that was, with his wooden legs many, many feet long, and what excitement he caused the next day when he walked down our street tapping on upstair tenement windows, ours included. Come to think of it, my own children, for all their respectable upbringing, missed some fun. They went to our local fair each year, of course, but somehow I don't think they had the excitement that I had.

Before we left the fairground that night, Pratt took me along to the caravan owned by Mr Hancock; the interior of that alone would have been worth a visit to the fair, so bright and shining and picturesque it was, though I have long since forgotten the details of the furnishings.

That night a rumour spread like wildfire through the town that a lion had escaped. Hair-raising stories were told of people having to climb lamp-posts in their efforts to get out of danger quickly, just as the lion was about to spring. We never discovered if there was any truth in the stories, for the fair moved away next morning; but the terror while it lasted was very real, and I believe many people bolted their doors more tightly than usual in case the lion should drop in to supper.

Talking of rumours, I remember the wildest rumours used to run through our street. I was never allowed out to play with other children, so it was not from them I heard these things. I always listened intently to grown-ups talking, and sometimes another tenant would drop in with the air of one who had great tidings to tell, and one would hear the strangest stories of a baby being born a few doors away with a horse's head, or with two heads, or of some monster up at the hospital being born with ten legs. Always the grown-up would shake her head wisely and say, 'Of course, they'll smother it.'

44

These sort of conversations would puzzle me greatly, while the bit about the smothering would make me feel sick and faint. If I tried to question Mrs Pratt afterwards I should be told, 'Little girls should be seen and not heard.' Thank God such ignorance as this is no more.

CHAPTER 5

Dusty, the Sword-Swallower

ONE DAY WHILE OUT WITH THE ORGAN WE CAME UPON A crowd of people, in the centre of which stood a ginger-haired man with the hilt of a sword just showing above his face as his head was tilted backwards. Pratt stopped to let me stand on the shaft to get a good view. He knew the man, for he said: 'Why, there's Dusty Brown, the sword swallower!' We stood looking at the scene while Dusty thrust one sword after another down that wonderful throat of his. After a while he laid the last sword down and shouted: 'Now, ladies and gentlemen, I will stick needles of all sizes in my chest and will not draw one drop of blood.' The man was as good as his word, for in those needles went, one after the other, darning needles and sewing needles, rows and rows of them, and not one drop of blood did he shed. I heard people saying that the man had a false skin, but I got to know him very well later, and I don't think he had. And anyhow he could not have had a false throat. Now while the needles were still in his chest the man sent round his cap. Many people placed coppers in it and the crowd began to disperse. Pratt waited until the people had all melted away, and Dusty had put away swords and needles, then he went over to him. They stood talking for a while, then both men came over to the organ. 'Dusty is coming to live with us,' he said simply.

Pratt put up the organ in some hired place near home (my dear friend Neddy was no longer with us), then we all three went in together. As we entered the room, Pratt said to his wife: 'I've brought Dusty Brown to live with us, instead of his going to a lodging-house. He's left his wife and kids.'

I do not remember that Mrs Pratt looked or expressed any surprise, nor was there any comment about sleeping arrangements. Her jaw (always square) was, if anything, a little squarer than usual, but she held her tongue and got the usual supper of cheese and bacon. This time a little more water was added. 'Go out and get me another loaf of bread, Emma,' she said, and added, 'Tell them not to forget the overweight.'

I fetched the bread and took it home intact with the overweight, for I could not eat it on the way, seeing Mrs Pratt had specially mentioned it. When I came in, she said as she filled the kettle, 'Now get some water.' She banged the can down with a clatter as she spoke.

I was very tired, for I had done a lot of walking that day. I picked up the can with a submissive 'Yes, Ma,' and proceeded down the stairs and out through to the backyard. I hated that yard; the lavatories were out there and they smelt beery and horrible.

Slop, slop, went the water on each step, as with two hands I lifted the can. An elderly man living on the top floor met me as he was coming down.

'Here, let me have that,' he said. He then walked right into the room with it. Looking at the two men, he said, 'What's wrong with you that the kid's got to fetch that can up the stairs?' He was gone before they could answer.

Pratt and his wife ate from the same plate as usual. Dusty, who was himself doing full justice to this unusual meal, kept glancing at them with more surprise, if that were possible, than I had looked at him earlier in the day as he swallowed the swords and became a human pin-cushion.

Mrs Pratt finished her supper. 'Come on, Emma,' she

said, starting to untie my various strings at the back, 'it's bedtime.'

Soon I was fast asleep. I was used to the bugs now – at least they no longer seemed to bite, or tickle, or whatever the beastly things do to the uninitiated; but I could never get used to the horrible smell. I had learned though to leave them alone. No squash – no smell.

So, as I have said above, soon I was fast asleep. When I awoke it was morning, and there, where Charlie's head had lain, and so puzzled me once before, the ginger head of our new lodger lay, but not asleep. The man was silently regarding me, and his look was not pleasant to see. Mrs Pratt soon rose. She sat on the edge of the bed as she always did while putting on her stockings. She never wore a nightgown, and nobody thought it strange that she should dress there with the lodger in the opposite corner of the room. As soon as she was dressed I also rose and, putting my bits and pieces on one by one, I then went over to her to have my strings tied.

The two men then rose and, having pulled on his trousers, Dusty said, 'I'll go down the yard and have a sluice if you don't mind.' Mrs Pratt silently and with set jaw handed him the grey family towel. When it was my turn to be wiped it was wetter than usual.

Dusty continued to live with us for a while and he continued to share my shakedown in the corner. While my purpose in writing this story is to deal with life as I found it, yet I shrink from making my little book sound more sordid than need be. I will therefore touch lightly on the subject by saying that he was not the sort of sleeping partner my Sunday School teacher would have chosen for me. The man was nasty. How could it have been otherwise? He would not have been there at all if he wasn't.

Dusty usually left the room when we did, he to go one way to give his sword-swallowing exhibitions and Pratt and I would go the other with the hurdy-gurdy.

I think we had another organ now, for the picture seems to be absent. Moreover the tunes were different. One tune I specially remember, for I was always hearing Pratt sing the words. I soon learnt them off by heart. Here it is:

Oh it's nice to have a home of your own,
And to sit by your own fireside,
If you've only got a table and a chair,
It's your own, and you're welcome there.
You're as good as anybody in the land,
As happy as a king upon his throne.
What more do you want
When you've got your wife and children
And a nice little home of your own?

The tune was catchy, and though I have never heard it since my childhood, how freshly it now springs to my mind. Another tune I remember was an Irish air. I know this now because I occasionally hear it on the wireless in 'Those were the days'. The tune is delightful, but I never heard the correct words. The only words I ever heard were obscene. I sang them because I heard other people singing them. I hadn't the faintest notion of what they meant. I wish now when I hear the tune on the wireless that I had not got such a retentive memory.

One day I heard Dusty ask Pratt if he could teach the little maid to swallow swords. Pratt raised no objection. The man called me over to the table in the centre of the room, and upon which he had laid swords of all sizes, and said, 'Look, I'll teach you to swallow this little one first. It will bleed a bit at first,' he warned, then added, 'but that will soon heal up, and after that I'll teach you to swallow the big ones.'

I looked at the man fearfully, not knowing what to believe, for after all I had seen him swallow the things and *he* didn't bleed.

'Hold your head back,' he commanded. 'Now open your

mouth wide – wider – that's it.' He raised the small sword over my mouth, but just as he was going to lower it down my throat, my terror knew no bounds. I shrieked, 'I shan't, I shan't!' I screamed. 'Leave her alone, Dusty,' Mrs Pratt said, simply but firmly.

Dusty put away the swords, greatly to my relief. I was half afraid now that he would want to turn me into a human pincushion, or should I say a cushion for needles. Instead he said, 'I tell you what, you come out with me this afternoon and I'll mesmerize you. That'll draw the crowds,' he said, turning to Pratt. Again Pratt raised no objection, but continued reading his paper in silence. Mrs Pratt got busy with the frying-pan.

'Will it hurt?' I asked Dusty anxiously. 'Lord bless you, no!' he replied. 'I shall just tell you to go to sleep and you will shut your eyes, then when I clap you will open them, that's all.'

It sounded simple enough, and as Pratt did not want me that day I accompanied Dusty.

We reached the place where Dusty intended to make his pitch, then he started shouting to the passers-by: 'Ladies and gentlemen, I will now put this little girl to sleep; at the word of command she will sleep until I clap my hands, then she will wake up. Watch, ladies and gentlemen, watch carefully.' He put his arm round my shoulder to support me, then said the word 'Sleep'. I shut my eyes, screwing them up tight. Dusty clapped and I said, 'Wait a minute, I haven't been to sleep yet.'

The crowd laughed and jeered, then melted away without throwing any coppers. Dusty was mad with me and took me home in disgust.

The man made no further attempts to educate me in the arts by which he procured a living. Soon after this, Dusty left us.

CHAPTER 6

A Salvation Army Home

IN THE WINTER EVENINGS PRATT AND HIS WIFE WOULD SIT AND solemnly play dominoes. Sometimes we would all three play 'Snap', when I got wildly excited, often knocking my orange box over in my eagerness to be the first to shout 'Snap'. As I have already said, I was never allowed out to play, so I thought a good deal of this evening relaxation round the table.

Sometimes I was awakened late at night by the drunken shouts of a man lurching heavily up the stairs. My heart would beat rapidly on these occasions, for it was not unknown for this to be followed by a crash overhead, as if the drunkard had knocked over a table full of crockery. Sometimes a piercing scream rang out.

In the morning one might catch a glimpse of the drunkard's wife with one, or perhaps two, black eyes. Yet if one met the same man when sober he would be as pleasant as possible.

Street fights were very common in our poor part of the town, and I don't know how my dear, gentle grandmother, who then lived a few doors away, could have borne it after her life at Redruth Church town. It was quite a usual thing to see a husband and wife knocking each other about in the street with a ring of spectators round them. I saw many such scenes from our window which was a tenement on the second floor.

From the remarks of grown-ups that I overheard, I gathered that it was never safe on these occasions to interfere on the wife's behalf for as likely as not she would turn round on the man or woman who was trying to do her a good turn.

One of these street fights led to a real tragedy. I'm glad to say I did not see it, but I heard people talking about it afterwards. The husband and wife were going hammer-and-tongs for each other, when a man set about the husband, telling him he ought to be ashamed to treat his wife in such a manner. Without a word that wife went indoors and brought out a flat-iron. Before anyone could stop her she had banged it down on the man's head. He was taken to hospital, and when the woman was charged with doing bodily harm to the man she said indignantly, 'Well, what right had he to interfere with my old man?'

I have seen drunken men carried away from such scenes by policemen, one at his head and one holding his feet. Such things always made me feel bad.

Even our mean street was transformed in that summer of 1902 just before King Edward's coronation, while the slightly more respectable street round the corner was a joy to behold. Gay bunting was looped across the street from window to window; boxes of gay flowers were to be seen everywhere. No matter where one went with the hurdy-gurdy, all was brightness and gaiety; Union Jacks were flying everywhere. Lord Kitchener's name was on everyone's lips, and whenever one listened to the newspaper being read aloud it seemed to be all about him. The war in South Africa was over and everybody was pleased about it, especially, I should think, the publicans, judging from the noise below in our street nightly. I can still hear drunken voices bawling along the pavement:

> '*Lord Roberts, and Kitchener,*
> *General Buller, and White,*
> *All went out to South Africa*

> *To have a jolly good fight.*
> *Now the war is over,*
> *Oh how happy I'll be,*
> *For I love sweet Rosy O'Grady,*
> *Sweet Rosy O'Grady loves me.'*

Then suddenly everybody was sorry again, for there was now to be no coronation after all – at least not yet – for the King was ill.

I managed to visit my grandparents on rare occasions, but dear grandmother, though not old according to our present standards (for she was only fifty-three when she died) was failing fast. She had borne much hardship and sorrow all her married life. She was not, I think, really fitted for such a hard existence, for she had been brought up in a comparatively well-to-do home. Her people were farmers. When, so soon after her marriage, bad luck came and her good-looking miner husband lost his sight, she did not complain on her own account, but set herself bravely to the task of being as good a mother and wife as was possible under the circumstances. It must always have been a losing battle. Now she was sinking rapidly – even my young eyes could see that – and it made me sad. Her sight at this time was almost gone, and she was often in great pain. Sometimes on our return from our hurdy-gurdy expeditions I would see Grandfather standing, tall and erect, under the railway arch where somebody had led him, and from which he was conducted later on in the day. Always he wore a notice around his neck on which was stated the cause of his loss of sight. Boot and shoe laces would be dangling from his left hand, while a tin cup was held in the other. As I recall the picture of that dear pathetic figure, I feel even at this age as if I want to weep.

It was some time after the Coronation, when one day from our window I saw a cab stop outside the house where my grandparents lived. Men were carrying a burden which they placed with difficulty into the car, then one of the men helped Grandfather in. While I pondered as to what it all meant, Mrs Pratt came over to the window. 'Your gran's going to hospital,' she said.

It was not many days later when my attention was attracted by a large glass coach down in the street. Black plumes waved on each of the four corners. I watched in silence as a coffin 'was placed inside. My grandfather was helped into a cab behind it. The man helping him was Auntie Susan's sailor husband whom I knew by sight. He and Auntie Susan then entered the cab. There was yet another cab; Auntie Anne and her husband got into that. Mrs Pratt stood beside me. 'Your gran's dead,' she said simply. I stood, and as the carriage passed slowly by, I just stared at them. 'H'm, you don't seem to care much,' Mrs Pratt said. I continued to stare out of the window – tears would not come. *Not then.*

After Grandmother's death my grandfather went to live with Aunt Anne some streets away. Before he left, however, a message came one day that my mother had come home from the Isle of Wight to see Grandmother before she died. She had come too late, and was now in Grandfather's room nursing her latest baby. She wished to see me.

I went in and stood shyly by her chair, feeling ill at ease, for it was a very long time now since I had met her. 'Hallo, Emma,' she said, then, uncovering the baby's face, she invited me to kiss 'my little brother.' I did so. 'Haven't you got a kiss for me?' she asked. I kissed her coldly. She meant nothing to me.

Soon after this I heard that she and her husband had come back to Plymouth to live, bringing the three children with them, that is, Harry and the baby, also another little boy between.

One day Mrs Pratt sent me out after the usual cheese and bacon scraps. They were all tiny bits, and the grocer placed them in a paper bag. Just as I was about to leave the shop a horse and trap came dashing along at great speed. The animal had taken fright at something or other, and in a moment I saw it crash into a nearby shop. Nobody was hurt except the poor horse itself which now lay in the road badly injured. A crowd collected and soon a very distressed man came up and knelt down by the horse's head. He was obviously the owner of the animal, and we could see he was greatly upset. After a while the crowd was told to stand back, and I saw somebody with a gun. The next moment there was a shot, and the injured horse lay still. Naturally I felt frightened and upset about the whole thing and had quite forgotten the bag of bits under my arm. When I got home Mrs Pratt scolded me for being so long. Then she said, 'Where's the cheese and bacon.'

I looked at the paper bag. I had been carrying it upside down and it had come open gradually. I had been spilling the contents on the ground as I walked sadly along thinking about the poor horse. Now the bag was practically empty. Mrs Pratt gave me one look – her face was livid. 'Take your kit and go,' she said.

I was just nine years old – I had nowhere to go. Nor, if it came to that, had I got any kit.

I stood a moment later on the pavement outside crying softly. It had all happened so quickly I was hopeless and bewildered. Where, oh where could I go? Somehow I found my way at length to the house where Grandfather was now living with Auntie Anne. They gave me a meal but could not keep me. Auntie Anne then took me to Maud, who as I have stated was now living again at Plymouth. Maud (or as I shall now call her, Mother) said she couldn't keep me, but she decided I'd best stay there for the night while she could think what to do with me.

When my stepfather came in she told him what had happened, and added quickly, 'I'll find somewhere to put her tomorrow.'

Mother cooked some fish for the evening meal. Harry (to whom now I was a stranger) and Willie (my stepfather's eldest boy) sat round the table with Mother and her husband.

Each was served. I patiently sat on an orange box away from the table, looking with hungry eyes at the food, but quite accepting the fact that I didn't belong.

Presently, as if in pity, my mother broke off a little of her own fish, then, placing it on a piece of bread, handed it to me, saying, 'Here, Emma.' I took the morsel, hungrily, gratefully.

My stepfather was in a bad temper. My presence in his home disturbed him. After the meal he went out and we saw no more of him until late that night I was awakened by his heavy, lurching footsteps as he staggered drunkenly into the room.

My mother had made me a shakedown in the corner of the room. In this I trembled as high words followed between them, in which the two names that were repeated most were those of 'Cod Murphy' – the name I knew that was my father's – and my own name. Presently the baby wakened. My mother took it up to feed it, and at last all was still.

When I awakened in the morning my stepfather had already left for work. Harry and little Willie came in from the next room in their little shirts, and Mother dressed them.

The presence of the children made a real family atmosphere, and although the home was barely and poorly furnished owing to my stepfather's fondness for drink, yet I longed then with a great longing to be one of the family, and to be able to call this home. Moreover, my mother's likeness to her own mother as I gazed at her feeding the baby brought a lump to my throat.

Mother continued to feed the infant. She had made a pap of bread and milk on a saucer, which she kept stirring about with a teaspoon; then she would put each teaspoonful into her own mouth to make it the right consistency before putting it into the baby's mouth. (This was a supplement to and *not* a substitute for breast feeding.) That, according to modern standards, must have been a dreadful thing to do. I often thought of it when I became a mother myself and was so fussy and particular about standards of cleanliness with bottles, etc. Yet I am bound to admit that my own mother's children came on far better in infancy than my own did at a later date, for all my modern ways.

Presently my mother told me to get up. 'I'm going to take you to the Salvation Army Home,' she said.

Later that day my mother rang the bell at the Home. It stood at the very end of the street I had been living in with Mrs Pratt. I had often passed it. A middle-aged officer answered the door. My mother begged that I might be taken in as she was too poor to keep me.

It was not long before I was wallowing luxuriously in a hot bath; my hair, which had been neglected, was cleansed, some clean clothing was brought into the bathroom and measured for size, and presently I was led to a room where there were people of all ages. There were about half a dozen children (little girls); the rest of the community ranged from twenty or thereabouts to women of seventy or even older. A contented atmosphere seemed to be in the room. I was, I think, given a little sewing to do, or try to do, for I had never learned to sew.

Presently a bell went, and everybody rose. We trooped into the dining-hall, where there were long tables upon which large plates of bread and butter were placed. There were also a few dates on each plate. As we took our places the officer in charge made a sign and everybody fell silent. Then Grace was sung:

> Be present at our table, Lord,
> Be here and everywhere adored,
> These creatures bless and grant that we
> May feast in Paradise with Thee.

Then there was a great scraping of chairs, and everybody fell upon the food. I believe I ate as though I were starving. The bread and butter may have been bread and margarine – I

57

don't know; I only know it tasted good to me, while as for the dates – this seemed the height of luxury.

After tea an officer came to fetch me. She said, 'I want to try a hat and coat on to you, for you will go to school tomorrow.'

My third attempt at going to school was a success. Clean and tidily dressed, my awful sense of inferiority was lifted, and though I certainly felt out of it all where lessons were concerned, my teacher was patient and helpful. Besides, I had the other home children to go to school with and to mix with at playtime. We were not dressed in any sort of home uniform, so that we were not obviously home children.

We had a considerable walk to school, and I had to pass the house where Mr and Mrs Pratt lived, but I saw nothing of them.

The Home was bright and cheerful. We children slept together in a large bright room. We each had our own bed, locker, brush and comb. For the first time in my life, as far as I could remember, I wore a nightgown; going to bed was a real luxury except that we were put to bed very early while we still wanted to play.

There were prayers each morning after breakfast. This I specially loved; the singing was bright, and the individual prayers in which God was always very earnestly beseeched to guide, bless and help us through our day's business whether it be school, work or play, made me feel good.

Saturday evening was mending-time. I was taught to darn my stockings; at least an attempt was made to teach me. Everyone was given mending to do. Then clean linen would be given round for the following day.

On Sundays we went in the morning to the nearest Salvation Army hall, where I much enjoyed the band and the bright services. Later in the day the-grown ups had *The War Cry* to read. We children had *The Young Soldier* with its simple stories and pictures.

In the afternoon the children gathered in a small room

around a table on which was a red cloth and a large open
Bible. This was called our Sunday School class. Here I was
an attentive and apt pupil. Soon I had learned by heart the
old, old stories of the Old Testament so beloved by children;
and once again I listened eagerly to the story of God's love for
children, as I had done in the Sunday School at Penzance. I
don't think Mrs Pratt had sent me while living in Plymouth;
if she did I do not remember it. I can still in fancy hear our
voices at the Sunday School class, as we sang that sweet old
hymn:

> *I think when I read that sweet story of old,*
> *When Jesus was here among men,*
> *How He called little children as lambs to his fold:*
> *I should like to have been with Him then.*
>
> *I wish that His hand had been placed on my head,*
> *That His arm had been thrown around me,*
> *That I might have seen His kind look when He said*
> *'Let the little ones come unto me.'*
>
> *Yet still to His footstool in prayer I may go*
> *And ask for a share of His love;*
> *And if I now earnestly seek Him below*
> *I shall see Him and hear Him above.*

If the reader dubs me as sentimental in that I speak of
my love for this old children's hymn, let him or her try to
imagine themselves in my place – uncared for, and unloved,
with not one spot of earth to which I had a right – then see if
these tender lines would not have an appeal to the heart that
nothing in after-life could obliterate.

On Sunday evening there was always a service in one
of the rooms in the Home. Chairs would be placed in rows.
The children sat in front. A row of chairs was placed to
face us. This, at the end of the service, became the penitent

form. The service would be taken by one or two officers, and although we had no band as we did at the hall, it was all very bright and earnest.

The food at the Home was excellent. We had well-cooked porridge each day with a generous helping of brown sugar and milk for breakfast. Plenty of bread and butter followed. Dinner was good and was always well cooked. For tea there was usually something that appealed to one's appetite – if not dates, then something else.

The Home had a steam laundry, and we children on Saturdays or in holidays usually went over for an hour or two just to rub collars or some such light duty. I don't think it did us any harm.

At Christmas we had a grand time. At the bottom of each child's bed on Christmas Eve a stocking hung just as it would do in any good family. And Santa Claus remembered us.

We were also taken to the beach sometimes, and on Bank Holidays everybody in the Home would have the opportunity of going to some pleasure spot accompanied by an officer.

We had a swing in the yard, and many happy times I had with the other children.

We had certain duties to fulfil on Saturday morning, such as rubbing up the wooden-handled forks, and wasn't the officer in charge of these things particular! Woe betide you if a bit of brickdust was left between the prongs! Another child would be given a tin of paste to clean the lavatory and bathroom taps. With what pride we made them shine! Yet another would be set to dust chairs, etc.

Then, quite suddenly, after a few months of this, it all came to an end.

One day I was taken by an officer back to my mother. Mother looked pleased to see me for one fleeting moment, but the smile faded as the officer explained they could not keep me any more for I had done something very naughty.

What, oh *what* could my crime have been, that the Salvation Army turned its back upon me? All my life I have pondered over this, and can find no answer.

It was only yesterday, as I was writing this book, that a suspicion of the truth came to my mind. The reader will recall that I spoke of an old Irish air that Pratt used to play on the hurdy-gurdy, and that the only words I had ever heard to it were obscene. I, as I have said, sang them because everybody else sang them, but did not have the faintest idea of what they meant. Now – I wonder – could I possibly have sung this song to the other children? It is sadly possible. If I *did*, then no wonder I was turned away. And yet – and yet – I was, after all, only nine, and they might have known I didn't understand what I was doing. Then again, it might not have been that. I wonder . . . I wish I knew.

Looking back, I think it was fortunate that I had not become deeply attached to any one particular officer, or my suffering at the change would have been much greater than it was. As it was, I had liked them all in a general sort of way, except perhaps one who was a bit grim-faced and whom I feared a little.

If this book should ever be read by the social workers of the Salvation Army, I would stress the fact that my memories of the home are only happy ones, and I am grateful that for a time at least I was cared for, washed, fed, made happy with the companionship of other children, a good clean bed in bright surroundings, and, above all, the simple religious teaching that was such a helpful memory in after-days. Here, then, let me say, 'Thank you.' I hold no grudge against you that I was turned away; I must have deserved it, and no doubt it was in the interests of other children – I don't know. But, to quote the title of a song that became popular a few years back –'Thanks for the memory' . . .

61

CHAPTER 7

Trudging the Roads Again

THE BABY, WHO WAS BEING NURSED ON MY MOTHER'S KNEE AS we entered, regarded me solemnly – not a smile on its little face. I think the infant must have sensed in some way that I was to be the disturber of the family atmosphere.

'Won't you take her back again?' asked Mother anxiously, adding, 'My man won't have her here.'

'No, the adjutant said I must leave her here,' the officer replied firmly. She let go my hand, then departed.

Mother regarded me with a worried look on her face. 'I don't know what we can do with you,' she said. 'When my man comes in he'll kick up ructions.'

I hung my head, my lip trembled.

'Nobody will ever like you,' Mother then said. This remark completely opened the floodgates. I wept loud and long.

Once again I sat on an orange box hungrily watching the family at dinner. My stepfather had a large beef steak on his plate, which he ate with gusto. Mother and her children had some salt fish. Again, as the family started the meal, Mother broke off a small piece of fish for me, and as before placed it on a piece of bread and handed it to me with the words, 'Here, Emma'. I cannot recall that I felt in any way cheated or badly treated. I had been brought up to accept the fact that I didn't belong anywhere, and what my Mother gave me now I accepted gratefully as a kindness on her part. I did not presume to regard it as my right.

Mother said with a sigh when they were half way through the meal, 'I think I'll take Emma to Mrs Roberts. She might let her sleep with Annie.'

'Well, she'll have to go somewhere,' said my stepfather. 'She's not going to live here, that's certain.'

Once again Mother took me by the hand, and before long we were standing before a mean looking second-hand clothes dealer's in the same street where I had lived with Mrs Pratt and then at the Salvation Army Home. We went into the shop. 'Hullo, Maud,' Mrs Roberts said as she wrapped up and gave a small boy the threepenny pair of trousers for which he had asked. Then, before Mother could say anything she asked, 'Whose little maid is that? It's never Emma, is it?' Mother said it was, then for a moment motherly pride came uppermost and she said, 'Isn't she a fine girl now?'

They talked for a while about me, then Mrs Roberts agreed to take me in, for a time at least. 'She'll be company for Annie,' she said.

Behind the shop there was a cosy living room. Mrs Roberts led me in and said to her daughter Annie, who was several years older than I was but very tiny and frail-looking, 'Emma Smith is coming to live with us. Be kind to her.'

Once again I settled in, and was soon part of this little household. Mr Roberts was a rag-and-bone merchant, and the second-hand clothing in the little shop was pickings from the best of the rags. The little home itself however was quite respectable and both Mr and Mrs Roberts were good homely people.

I had the same food as the family. It was set out in the little living room, the table properly laid, and meals were regular. Annie was a friendly girl; her sister was a good deal older and had left home long ago. The girl now was glad to have a companion, and she shared whatever she had with me.

We slept together in a large bed which Annie had in the old days shared with her sister, and the room was her own.

Though her father was only a rag-and-bone merchant, the girl seemed to me to possess many girlish treasures. This was the very same family that had taken my grandparents in when we first came to Plymouth, only then they lived in a much better part of the town and had not then got the rag-and-bone business. Mrs Roberts had been a dear friend of my grandmother's many years before, when she also lived at Redruth Church town. Now I feel sure she had taken me in for the old friendship's sake.

Alas, I had not been with this good family hardly any time at all when one morning Mrs Roberts was horrified to find me covered with a rash.

'Emma has got scarlatina,' she said to her husband.

'Then she must go back to Maud at once, before she gives it to Annie,' her husband replied.

'Well, I expect Annie will get it now anyway,' Mrs Roberts said, upset.

'Well, Maud is her mother and must look after her,' Mr Roberts said decidedly. His wife agreed. 'Come, Emma,' she said; 'I must dress you and take you to your mother.'

I was too ill to care much where I was going or what was going to happen to me. I should think I must have found that walk difficult, but it is one of those things I cannot remember. My next memory seems to be of Mother's living room once again. Here I was put in a shakedown in the corner.

Then my stepfather came in later on. He didn't say much at first when he saw me and realized I was ill, but when one of his own children approached me and childishly offered me a biscuit, his wrath knew no bounds. He jumped up and with one almighty kick, over went the table, the few crocks and all. The crash was fearful.

'Take her out of here,' he commanded.

Poor Mother – it is only as I write that I realize what a

time she must have had. 'All right, Jack,' she said, trembling, 'only don't go on so.'

Now in the tenement house where Mother was then living, there was at that time an empty room upstairs. Somehow Mother procured the key to this room, but feared the landlady would find out. She then transferred my shakedown to the corner of this room, and I lay down.

I have never forgotten that long, long night. But before night came there were weary hours to toss and turn alone in this strange room surrounded by four walls only. I suppose I must have slept by fits and starts. Presently I heard a clatter of a water-can down in the yard. It was, I thought, morning, and now at last I should see somebody and could ask for a drink. I got up and went over to the window. There was Harry standing by a water-can waiting for it to be filled. I banged on the window to attract his attention. He looked up.

'Is it morning?' I called as well as I could.

'No,' said Harry, 'we haven't been to bed yet.'

'I want a drink,' I called, my heart sinking to think that I had the long night in front of me, before I was fetched away to the hospital as Mother had said I should be.

The long night came and somehow went. The next day a van came for me, and I was wrapped in a red blanket and placed in the van that contained two other little girls besides a nurse. I sat in the red blanket, so did one of the other girls. The third (another Emma) lay on a stretcher and was considered to be very ill indeed. Both these children were placed in the same ward as myself.

Those few weeks at the fever hospital are among my brightest memories. Only one thing mars it; Emma Lee, the little girl that was lying in the ambulance at the time I was fetched, died after a few days. We saw her sorrowing parents (who looked comfortably-off people) stand by her bedside at the last. Child as I was, I puzzled my head a great deal about that. Why, oh why, did this other Emma whose mother and father wanted her so much, have to die, while I, whom nobody wanted – not even my mother – had to get better and live? Besides, I was very religious at heart, and was always wishing I could go to heaven, where I had been assured so often in Sunday School that there was room for all.

Emma Lee was taken out of the ward, and I suppose my attention was distracted by other matters. Things which I suppose other children took as a matter of course were to me a great novelty. Toys there were in plenty, and that (to *me*) greatest of all joys – picture books.

For some unknown reason I became rather a favourite with the nurses, especially our night nurse. When I was able to get up, she allowed me to do many little helpful jobs which gave me a sense of importance. This, to a child who all her life had laboured under a feeling of inferiority, was good.

What fun we had when, soaking our feet to remove dead skin, several of us sat round the edge of the bath, and how we would splash and chuckle with laughter! There was a stream in the grounds by which we played, taking tadpoles out of the water when nobody was looking. The Matron saw us doing this one day and told us we should give the poor things scarlet fever. I didn't know if she was in earnest or not.

There was a plantation with a wall, over which sometimes the heads of unofficial visitors would appear. One day I heard my own name called, and there was Mother's head. She threw me down a bag of sweets. She had no right to pay such a visit, yet it is comforting to reflect that she had thought about me.

Alas, all good things in my life came to an end far too quickly, and the inevitable day came when I had to be 'put up'. This meant I had to lie in bed with the bottom of the bedclothes turned back to show my feet, waiting for the Doctor's inspection. He came – I passed – and once again I was doomed to enter the cold inhospitable world.

I was sitting in a small room waiting for my mother.

I had been bathed and disinfected, and in company with several others had sat in this room covered with a red blanket until called for. The Matron had told me that my mother had been given a guinea to buy me new clothing, so that I ought to be well set up.

Everybody else had long ago left. I sat alone, wondering and worrying. Just suppose nobody ever fetched me, what then? Where could I go – and in a blanket! Now and then a happy thought would cross my mind, that when Mother did appear I should have nice new clothes. Daylight was fading when at last she put in an appearance. She explained that she had had to meet her man who had that day come out of prison where he had been for some days for being drunk and disorderly. The news left me quite indifferent. Prison seemed to me a household word. What did interest me was the bundle of clothing. I waited breathlessly while she undid the bundle. There was nothing new; to make matters worse my boots were too tight and I was very uncomfortable. I started to weep, and Mother thought it was because I had not been fetched earlier. She was on the defensive at once. 'Look, Emma,' she said, 'my man comes first. I had to meet him, and I couldn't be here as well, could I?' 'No,' I said, trying hard to stop the flow of tears. She never knew that I had heard about that guinea, or what a disappointment I had undergone.

Again the shakedown in the corner of Mother's living-room was my bed. Everything had been disinfected after I had been sent to hospital, and mercifully the other children had not taken my fever, not even the little brother who had offered me the biscuit. I remember how overwhelmed with relief I had been about this, as my stepfather's awful wrath at the time had filled me with a terrible fear that the child might get ill and perhaps die, and that if he did it would be all my fault. My stepfather must have given me that impression for it to be such an overwhelming fear.

I could only have been with the family a day or two when, feeling very miserable, I made my way to the Salvation

Army Home. I sat on the front doorstep for some time, waiting, waiting for that door to be opened.

At last it was opened, and the officer of whom I had stood a little in awe stood there.

'Hullo, Emma,' she said. 'What are you doing here?'

'I want to come in,' I replied.

'Oh no, Emma, you've had your chance,' the officer replied firmly. She closed the door.

It was, I think, only a day or two I had been with Mother and her little family, just long enough for the impression of the room to be fixed in my mind, the memory of fear at my stepfather's lurching, drunken footsteps in the evening, and the inevitable high words before everything settled down for the night. Always my name was the word most mentioned on these occasions.

There was a candle factory near. The smell of that is fixed in my mind also, for it used to make me feel ill, and I would hold my breath while I ran past.

The children interested me. Harry I knew to be my own special brother in a way the others weren't, but even he was separated from me in that he sat at table with the others, and bore the surname of O'Brien, while I bore that of Smith (for I had now taken my own name again, whereas when I was living with the Pratts I had been known as Emma Pratt).

After a short while Mother said to me one day: 'Would you like to go back to Mr and Mrs Pratt? They are going travelling again, through Cornwall, and they want to take you.'

Now the reader would expect me to decline with horror after all I have written. The truth was, I pondered in silence for a while, as I considered the position. I was not wanted here; I only added to my mother's troubles by causing more friction between her and her husband. There were no pretty gardens hereabouts to be seen as there would be when travelling. All I could remember was variety, glasses of milk, generous slices of cake, kindly words of householders. If I remembered my vague worry and misery at Pratt's behaviour when we were alone, I must have pushed it from me.

'I'll go,' I said.

Mother looked relieved. 'Come on, then,' she said.

'Take off your hat and jacket, Emma,' said Mrs Pratt as I entered the door with Mother. That was the only greeting.

The two women talked for a while, then Mother left. Before she left she kissed me lightly. 'Goodbye, dear. Be a good maid,' she said.

That night I renewed my acquaintance with my old enemy the bug, but shut my eyes tight and gave myself up to looking forward to cottage gardens, glasses of skimmed milk, slices of cake, raw turnips in the fields, animals and birds of the farmyard. Pratt's loathsome behaviour, blistered heels, and the like, were banished firmly from my thoughts.

Once again we set out with the hurdy-gurdy, our destination for that night being Saltash.

I was older now, nearing ten years of age, as far as I can make out. Pratt had nailed a strap to the organ shafts. This I had to put myself into, and as Pratt himself walked between the shafts where in the old days Neddy used to be, I helped pull as I walked in the strap. Sometimes I was relieved by Mrs Pratt.

On the way to Saltash we stopped as before at wayside cottages and farms. Sometimes we played the organ, at others we sang well-known hymns from Sankey and Moody. Mrs Pratt had a book of these hymns which she used, and her voice was fairly good. I very soon learnt them all by heart. Many, of course, I had learned previously at the Salvation Army Home and at Sunday School in Penzance.

So we continued on our way, and if I did not find quite the same compassion now that I had found when younger, people were still good to me; and, true to my expectations, I found the same generous hospitality in the matter of skimmed milk, cake, and bits and pieces of clothing – perhaps a pair of boots and stockings. I don't mean that clothing was showered upon me, but somehow just when one's stockings and perhaps undergarments became uncomfortable, some kind-hearted woman would notice and supply me with fresh.

We continued our journey from Saltash to Callington, from Callington to Liskeard, from Liskeard to Bodmin, from Bodmin to St Austell, from St Austell to Truro, from Truro to Redruth, my own birthplace. How I longed to see that dear cottage of Grandmother's again! But it was not to be. Once again we took the route that did not lead through Church Town, though I had begged and prayed Mr Pratt to go that way. From Redruth we travelled to Hayle and from Hayle on to our final destination, Penzance. I do not remember just how long the journey took in all. Sometimes it was wet; then we would have to stay at lodgings for that day, or even perhaps for two. So the length of journey, or rather the length of time the journey would take, depended very much upon weather conditions.

At each of the various lodging-houses I had slept as hitherto at the foot of Mr and Mrs Pratt's bed. If this had been uncomfortable before, the reader will readily understand that it was doubly so now that I was older and so much bigger.

It was autumn at the time of this journey, and as we drew near to Penzance darkness fell. We trudged along in silence; I was very tired as always at the end of the day's journey. The lights of the distant town looked very friendly and inviting. These are tame words to use and do not express at all the thrill that those lights gave me. Nearer and nearer they came. At last – at long last – we reached the edge of the town. To my disgust Pratt decided to sing at the first house we came to. After the first hymn he gave up the attempt for I could not sing a note I was so tired, also Mrs Pratt was anxious to get on to the lodging-house. We reached this haven at length. Our loft was let, but there was room for us inside, until such time as we found a small cottage, for this time the Pratts intended to settle at Penzance indefinitely.

The lodging-house was, as before, full of Italians, some of whom we had met before. The common-room was cosy and warm, and there was the inevitable smoke haze and smell of cooking.

I think Pratt must have sold the organ to one of the lodgers, for we did not use it again.

Once again I started to go to school. St Mary's was a Church School for girls. I liked the school at once, and always the teachers were kind to me, for all my neglected appearance. I was, of course, very backward at school on account of all the time I had missed, but for all that I became aware, by remarks I overheard, that I was looked upon as being intelligent. I did not know at the time I heard this what the word intelligent meant; I hoped, however, that it was not anything bad. I didn't think it could be, because the headmistress and teacher who were discussing me looked kind as it was said.

We lived for some time at the lodging-house. During this time I amused myself greatly mimicking sounds and gestures of the Italian lodgers. At school in the playground I would draw quite a crowd of girls around me while I gabbled and used my hands expressively. I really believed I was speaking Italian. So did my hearers, and after a time other children would say when they saw me approaching, 'Here comes that old Eytalian maid'; just as in my younger days at Redruth other children would say, 'Here comes that old Union maid'. Often, too, when living in Plymouth, I have heard myself referred to as 'that old hurdy-gurdy maid'. I have been many things, it seems, to many children.

I now gave myself (when I had the chance) wholeheartedly to my school work, taking a great interest in some things, if not in all. As time went on and more and more of my schoolfellows had seen me singing in the streets on Saturdays, the old feeling of inferiority crept over me miserably, for children began to shun me in the playground

71

and refer to me, not only as 'that old Eytalian maid', but 'that old maid that goes out singing'. Besides all this I was sent to school dirty and unkempt, and though for the most part my fellow pupils came from mean streets, there were exceptions, and even those from the mean streets were all, without exception, better dressed and cleaner than I was.

My schooling was frequently interrupted by Pratt keeping me away from school for a day's singing in the surrounding villages. We would in turn visit St Ives, Newlyn, St Just, Mousehole and Sennen Cove.

I was anxious to please my teacher and do well at school, yet there was something about these singing excursions that has had a grip on me all my life. The gardens were no longer attractive, for now it was winter. But those winter sunsets! The roar and splashing of sea waves, the glimpses of cosy interiors as a cottager would come out with a coin, the flicker of firelight, the walk at night in the dark under a clear starlight sky; then moonlight, on a night when full moon and clouds played hide and seek with each other!

Before writing this book, I always felt my young days were just bad and sordid all through; but as I write, much that was lovely has forced itself upon my memory.

Sometimes on the way home at night a horse and cart would come along the country road. Often I would be limping, sometimes Pratt would put up his hand and beg a lift, sometimes a kindly driver would stop of his own accord and offer us one. Oh, the blessed relief of getting off my feet with my blistered heels, when I could watch those stars or the cloudy moonlight in drowsy comfort.

Specially did I love a visit to St Ives. We would sing on the quayside, and pennies would come raining down at us; fishermen would give us something from their catch just as they did at Newlyn. As I write, I fancy I can hear the screeching of the gulls overhead. We would sit near the lifeboat house to eat our bread and cheese and drink tea from a bottle. As we ate, seagulls would swoop down, screaming, compelling one to share one's dinner. The waves would speak to me; they seemed full of messages.

As I am writing, the emotion that used to rise up within me as I gazed out to sea seems to come back afresh as I recall it all. Once before, when I was only six, I had been looking out to sea as Pratt and I sat together, and as I looked I saw the sky and sea meet, or so I thought. That, I decided, must be the end of the world. I was not very pleased with the world at that moment. 'When I grow up,' I said to Pratt, 'I shall sail right out there where the sky comes down into the sea, and I shall take a pin with me; I will then prick the sky with the pin, and the world will burst like a balloon. You'll see!' I added threateningly.

At St Ives there were quaint little shops in narrow cobbled streets. In the evening they were brightly lit; I suppose in these days we should think them dimly lit, but they seemed bright and cheerful then. A delicious smell of cooking would force itself upon us as we passed hotels where preparations for a meal were in progress. At times Pratt would call at the back door of one or other of these hotels and be given a large basin of dripping. I think we always carried a frail with us, both to carry our dinner of bread and cheese, and to put any possible gifts therein.

St Ives was farther away from Penzance than the other places that we visited. Moreover it was one of the two places that possessed a railway station, and though we walked one way, we came back by train.

Can the reader put himself in my place for a moment and imagine himself or herself at the age of ten, after a hard day's walking and singing, standing on a cliff making what was to be the last call of the evening, and looking down at the lights of the railway station, watching eagerly for the one-way train that would come puffing in from Penzance and would patiently wait until you had dashed down the hill just in time to catch it before it puffed its way back again. Oh, the thrill of that sight to a hungry, tired, footsore girl, such as I was!

Then, again, on the days that we walked to St Just, the cold winter morning air was exhilarating as I stepped out briskly before the blisters got bad; and as we sang before the row of cottages so near to the beach, the lap, lap, of the waves on the shingle would mingle with our voices as we sang the old hymns that these people loved. And on the way back we called at a large estate where the squire was well known for his generosity to the poor. We would do well there. I think I can recall that the old gentleman looked at me in a troubled way and asked why I was not at school, but Pratt gave some evasive sort of answer, and no more was said.

Then there would be a walk through the woods, and perhaps the moon chasing clouds overhead; then the loud hoot of an owl, then another – all these things thrilled me. Then Pratt would spoil it all – after which, all I would be conscious of were my sore feet and misery.

CHAPTER 8

School, Fair and Milk-Round

WE HAD LEFT THE LODGING-HOUSE NOW, AND WERE LIVING IN the slummiest street in the town. Our two-roomed cottage was situated in a court that, in spite of the fact there was not a flower to be seen, was dignified by the name of Strawberry Gardens.

The cottage had one small room up and one down. I cannot recall Mr or Mrs Pratt buying any furniture, so I think the bare necessities the cottage contained must have belonged to the landlord. Here for the first time while living with the Pratts I had a bed of my own; a ramshackle sort of bed certainly, but it was my own. Even here I was never allowed to play with other children.

The cottage was a tidy distance from the school, but I was a good riser, and when the town authorities started free breakfasts for the poor children of the town, I would rise and go off in the dark winter's morning and really enjoy doing it. The hall where the breakfasts were supplied was half-way between home and school, so it suited me well. Large plates of bread and butter and mugs of steaming hot cocoa would greet our eyes as we entered the hall, and I think I was able to concentrate on my lessons all the better for being well fed and warmed before the school began.

Prize-giving day at school caused me real heartache. To

75

see that pile of brightly coloured books, and to know that I who would do anything in the world to possess a book could not have one because I was always being kept away, was hard to bear. I looked with envious longing at the well-dressed prize-winners, both on account of the nice frocks they were wearing for this special occasion, but even more because of those books. Prize-winners would proudly pass their books round for non-prize-winners to admire. A lump would come into my throat and I could hardly bear to look.

On coming home one day from school, I saw a small book resting on the stone ledge beneath some iron railings, at the bottom of a cottage garden. I stood and battled with temptation; here was a book, small certainly, but still a book. Did it belong to anybody? Should I take it? Would it be stealing or not? How long I did battle with myself I don't know, but at last I could not struggle against temptation any longer. I took the book after furtively looking round to see if anybody was looking, then made a dash for home, feeling as if all the police in Penzance were after me. I reached home at last, dashed in and shut the door. Then and not until then did I open my precious book. It was 'words' – *nothing but words*. I shed tears of disappointment, and that, dear reader, is how I got my first dictionary. How trivial it all looks when in writing, in these days, when the poorest child can have its story and picture books even at an early age. I was ten, and had never possessed a book of my own, and I loved books. Trivial it may seem, but to me it was more important than I can tell you.

My class teacher, of whom I was very fond, held up twelve beautiful painting books for the class to see one morning, and she said: 'Now these twelve lovely painting books are to be given to twelve girls who come to school regularly for a whole month.' I had been excited when I first saw the books. On each page there were pictures of brightly coloured birds, on the opposite page there was an outline of the same birds all ready for colouring in by the lucky owners. When, however, Miss Joyce stated the conditions under which they were to be given, my heart sank. I knew perfectly well that I should never be allowed to go a whole month without having to go out singing.

Of course, my fears were justified, and to make matters worse, the books were presented to the fortunate winners on a day that I happened to be at school; that is – eleven of the books were given away. Miss Joyce held up the last book and, looking right into my eyes, she said: 'This last book is to be given to the girl who is the best behaved for one whole month.' I knew then that she intended that I should have the opportunity of winning one of those books. I would not let her down. Another month passed and – I got my book.

What a joy that book was! Even Mrs Pratt was glad for me, and spared a copper or two so that I could buy a cheap box of paints.

Christmas-time came. If I did not have a Christmas tree of my own, or very much in the way of presents, it was nevertheless a time of excitement. As I went singing round the different villages I was thrilled (though perhaps a bit envious as well) at the sight of many gaily decorated trees in cottage windows. People were unusually kind in the matter of coins and gifts of food, and on Christmas Eve one kind person presented me with a very nice blouse and skirt; these garments did not fit very well, but the colours made me very happy.

When I got home earlier than usual, Mrs Pratt took me down the main street of Penzance. There I enjoyed the sight of gaily dressed shops. Then we bought strips of coloured paper to make paper chains. Mrs Pratt made a paste of flour and we stuck our fingers into it (we did not rise to a brush); when we had made the chains we hung them across the living-room. The room was very poorly furnished, but those chains transformed it, so festive did they look. I believe those chains gave me more pleasure than the elaborate chains one buys today can ever give present-day children.

Most of my joy came from carol singing both at school

and in the streets, for I believed wholeheartedly in the Christmas story of Bethlehem. I caught a glimpse of so many decorated interiors and gaily decked Christmas trees, that I think I had my share of seasonable excitement.

'Emma,' said Mrs Pratt one day, 'I've promised Mr Penardo the dairyman that you should do a milk-round for him before and after school. He will give you a couple of coppers each day, and mind you bring them home.' 'All right, Ma,' I said, willingly. 'Besides the coppers,' she said, 'he will give you breakfast on Sunday morning. And,' she added, 'I bet he'll put cream in the basin of bread and milk that he says you will have.'

By this time the year was getting on and the free breakfasts that had been supplied during the winter months had now come to an end. The prospect of at least one good breakfast a week sounded good.

The next day I went to see the dairyman. He told me the streets and numbers of the houses at which I was to call each morning and evening. As I have already said, early rising was easy to me, so that presented no difficulty.

Big and strong though I was, that milk-can was terribly heavy to carry; I felt as if I was going all lopsided. One comfort, of course, was that every pint of milk I took out, it grew a bit lighter. I just could not help slopping the milk as the can kept banging against my leg, and I looked eagerly for the taps in customers' yards in those places where I called at the back doors, and if I could do so without being seen I would put the can under the tap and pour a little water in to make up for what I had spilled.

I soon got used to my streets and customers so that in a day or so I had no difficulty in keeping to the timetable.

How any of those customers could have allowed the delivery of their daily milk to be carried out by such an unkempt girl as myself I can't think, but so it was. I think I am right in saying I earned twopence a time. Usually I took my earnings faithfully to Mrs Pratt, but on one or two occasions I yielded to the temptation to buy sweets. Then there was ructions.

Whether the milk-round interfered with the singing expeditions or not I can't remember, but the work did not last very long. It may be that customers complained of water in the milk, or of the condition of the girl who delivered it. If they did, I could not blame them.

At school I progressed as far as it was possible for one who was so often absent. Reading I specially loved. Once a week we took it in turns to read aloud an interesting story book. How I looked forward to my turn! I always got full marks for clear, distinct pronunciation, and anything that helped me above my feeling of inferiority I am sure was good. I loved also – oh, how I loved – the smell of old books. Our history books were old, and to this day the smell of old books will take me back to those history lessons when I would lift the open book to my nose and draw in the scent with the same pleasure as one would a nosegay.

Arithmetic baffled me no end; yet I can remember just once getting full marks for having my sums right, and one extra for neatness. How I managed that has always been a mystery, for I am quite certain I never cribbed.

But though I did quite well in a few things and was, as I have said, considered by my headmistress and my own teacher to be intelligent, yet, alas, I could never make up for all I had lost, and I am quite sure that today a child of eight would shame me if we sat side by side and had the same lessons to do.

On very rare occasions Mrs Pratt would accompany Pratt and me as we went singing. She had a decent voice, so that she sometimes sang, but at other times she would play a jews' harp. I have not seen one for years, so perhaps my reader may not know what a jews' harp looks like. It was a small instrument that she put in her teeth; there was a spring in the centre, and this she would strike with her right thumb. It made a little musical sound which, however, used to set my teeth on edge.

One day when Pratt and I were visiting Mousehole, which was some seven or eight miles from Penzance, my heels became very blistered on the return journey, and I wondered how I'd reach home. We called at a farm-house, and after singing for a while the farmer's wife offered us some saffron cake and milk while the farmer himself gave us a whole shilling. This, of course, was rare.

'The little maid seems lame,' said the kindly man. 'How are you going to get back to Penzance tonight?'

'Well,' said Pratt, 'do you think we could sleep in your barn?'

The farmer scratched his head. 'Well, there's plenty of good straw in there,' he said. 'You'd be comfortable enough. Only mind you don't go striking matches.' Pratt promised he wouldn't, so the farmer said, 'All right then. After all, I don't see how the little maid can get home in that condition. Here, Mother,' he called over his shoulder to his wife, who had gone back into her kitchen, 'these travellers are going to sleep in the barn tonight. I was wondering if you could tend the poor little soul's feet for her. Then if she would like, to come down to chapel a bit later on. There's going to be a revival service this evening,' he said, turning again to Pratt.

That dear kind woman took off my boots and bathed my feet. Then she got a clean needle and pricked the blisters. She brought a pair of stockings and put a little clean rag in each heel, after putting some powder on it.

The chapel was quite close, and it soon became packed with villagers. The service began with the hymn 'Behold me standing at the door'.

I would give much to hear this old hymn sung again with the earnest heartiness it was sung that night in that little packed wayside chapel. The preacher was full of fiery zeal. He stamped up and down the rostrum, pleading, warning, encouraging; mostly, I think, warning. 'Hell' was the word that was used most often, at least it's the only one that stayed in my mind. I became full of fear – all those horrible indecencies of Pratt's crowded into my mind, for though I was innocent and could not help these things, yet it seemed to me that my soul was blacker than pitch. The preacher's eyes were like fire, they burnt into my very soul. I felt surely there was nothing hidden from this man. To hell I should go sure enough. I could, in imagination, almost hear the fat of my body hissing in those scorching flames, and then – to think it was to go on for ever and ever – was there never to be an end to it all – would I never get to the painless cinder stage? You may smile, dear reader, but to me it was a nightmare.

Presently the preacher's voice softened and he held out his hands pleadingly, as he implored us to turn from our sinfulness and live. It was all so easy; all one had to do apparently to avoid that awful burning process was to come out to the penitent form in front and to repent; then start afresh and lead good clean lives in future.

Need I say that I was one of the first to stumble towards that penitent form. Some good Christian soul came and knelt beside and asked me to tell him my troubles. Not one word could I say about what really was troubling me, but feeling that I must say something, I told of my keeping one or two of the pennies that I earned from selling milk. Nevertheless I poured out my trouble to my Maker in private.

After the service many people came round and spoke kindly to me. I felt good, clean, and full of determination that in future neither Pratt nor anybody else should rob me of my new-found joy. The farmer and his wife both congratulated me in a kindly fashion in that I had, as they expressed it, been 'saved' that night. Pratt seemed pleased of the notice that was showered upon me, and I think I was justified in thinking that he would in future leave me alone.

Alas for my comforting belief! Through the farmer's kindness we slept in the barn that night, and for all Pratt had seemed pleased at my being saved, he behaved in his usual way. When I tearfully pleaded with him and told him it was wrong, he simply said there was nothing wrong about it at all, and that God made us that way, and it was perfectly natural; but it would never do to talk about it, because people thought it was wrong.

Gone was my happy, clean-souled feeling after this, and I felt depressed and miserable.

The next morning Pratt decided that we might as well use the day as we were already several miles from home, so we worked our way round the coast to St Just. At every cottage that we sang, Pratt told of my conversion. He spoke as if he was proud of it, too. People were touched, and I am sure he got more money on account of it.

I felt more miserable than ever, and when I sang that pathetic old sacred song, 'When the dewy light was fading', I longed, with even greater intensity than usual, to be the 'Mary' of the song, to whom the angels said:

> Come, there's roam, yes there's room,
> Room in that glorified angel band.

When we reached home, Mrs Pratt cooked the cheese and bacon, and did not even ask 'Where did you sleep last night?'

The fair had come to Penzance. Pratt and I went to the entrance of the fairground, and sang to the people coming in and out. This kind of thing was always considered profitable.

Presently we saw a hurdy-gurdy coming towards us; the figure in the shafts looked vaguely familiar. Then, as he came closer, I recognized our one-time fellow-lodger, the owner of Bruce the monkey. Alas! I looked in vain for the little animal. There was no sign of him; instead, a bird's cage with a yellow canary hung in front of the organ. The man halted as he saw us, and as we were no longer rivals, having now no organ of our own, he condescended to speak.

The two men talked for a while, the Italian every now and then spreading out his hands expressively. The conversation seemed to be about Russians and Japs and war. When they ceased talking, I asked, 'Where's Bruce?' Bruce's one-time owner shrugged his shoulders and spread out his hands, while his face looked sad. Then he told me in broken English that Bruce had died the year before, having caught 'pomona', the result of a chill through being out in a violent storm.

I was sorry about the 'pomona', as everybody in my small world called pneumonia. Had the man told me the little monkey had busted himself with chip potatoes, I should not have been surprised.

Cheering up, the man opened the birdcage and, gently thrusting a little stick into it that he kept for the purpose, he drew the yellow canary out. The bird made no attempt to fly away. The owner talked to it, calling it 'My beauty', to which the bird chirruped. Then he replaced it in the cage and, picking up the shafts of the organ, proceeded farther along the road where he took up his pitch.

I felt quite sad for a while after this conversation, for I could not bear to think of the bright agile little monkey, who had made so many people laugh with his antics, dashing about in his little red cap and jacket, now lying cold and still.

As the tinny notes of the hurdy-gurdy came over the air, Pratt decided we had better move our pitch as we were too close to the organ. After a while we decided to give up any further attempt at singing, and great was my joy when he said we would now walk round the fairground.

This fair did not make the impression on my mind that the one I described earlier had done. One thing only stands out clearly. As we walked round gazing at the various attractions – coconut-shies, boat-swings, switchbacks and children's roundabouts, not forgetting the colourful Italian women with their gay head-dresses – I suddenly caught sight of a familiar figure, tall, erect, wearing a tin notice-board round his neck, boot and shoe laces dangling from his left hand, while he held a tin cup in the other. A boy stood beside him. I caught my breath with the wonder of it. Then I dashed over and threw myself upon my grandfather's neck with delight.

'Grandad, Grandad,' was all I was capable of saying, as the poor man looked startled at this sudden onslaught.

Then he got his breath back. 'Is that Emma?' he asked. 'Well, you nearly knocked me down,' he said, but he looked pleased all the same.

Pratt now came over and the two men exchanged greetings. Harry and I had very little to say to each other. We had grown apart and I think we were a little shy of each other. Grandfather said that he and Harry had come for the fair all the way from Plymouth by train, and he was going to find our cottage anyway before he returned, as he said he would not have gone back without visiting me.

Pratt said: 'Does it pay you and the boy to come all that way and put up in lodgings?'

'Yes,' Grandfather replied, 'for I shall collect more at the fair in one night than I should in several days under the arch. Even when you count the railway fares it pays to come; besides somebody I know is putting us up for two nights and she won't charge much.'

I have heard it said that blind men often collect more than they would earn if working. Well, I am quite sure it was not so with Grandfather, for he only barely paid his way. He was a good man of sober, temperate habits, and any money placed in that cup was spent wisely on food and other bare necessities of life. Rent had to be paid, and gas and firing; also even a blind man must have a change of clothing. In these days he would have had a pension of some sort, so that it would not be necessary to stand all hours with his hands in the same position as he did. Not until I started writing this book did I realize what a strain it must have been for the poor fellow always to stand in that same way, the right hand holding out the mug, the left holding the laces. There were bad days, when intense cold, rain, or snow, kept him indoors; so that when he could get out, what was placed in the tin mug had to tide him over those periods.

Grandfather was at this time living with one of his daughters, but he was not the sort to sit day in and day out in his armchair and be a burden to anyone.

Grandfather gave me a penny. 'Here, Emma, buy some sweets,' he said, feeling the coin carefully first of all to be sure of its value. I took the coin with excitement, for a penny of my own was riches.

We parted then for the night, but I promised to be at the railway station the following day to see him and Harry off. I kept my promise with Mrs Pratt's permission, and as the train steamed out of Penzance station, Harry and I waved to each other.

I did not see either of them again until years later.

My school life was taking great hold on me, and though it was impossible to make up for all the time I had lost, I was doing quite well in certain subjects.

I felt also that the head-mistress herself and my own class teacher liked and trusted me. I longed to be able to confide my worries to one or other of these two. Fear of Pratt, however, kept me silent, in addition to which I did not know how to express myself about the matter of his unnatural behaviour.

The street I lived in with the Pratts had a very bad name, and if at school any article was found to be stolen the children living in our street always became suspect – that is, strange to say, with one exception, and that exception was myself. I tell this in no boasting spirit. God knows I had nothing to boast about, but when one considers the sort of existence I led, I think it gratifying to remember that on the occasions when everybody living in our street was asked to stay behind for questioning, the teacher always said, 'except Emma Pratt, she may go home.'

There was to be a 'pageant' at school – at least I am not sure that 'pageant' is the correct name for this. Twelve girls of different ages were to take part. A song that we were learning and which I loved very much, was to be portrayed. How I longed to be in this lovely scene; I knew, however, that such a privilege could not be mine; for even if I could be certain of attending rehearsals, which I couldn't be, I knew that it would be impossible for me to own the white billowy dress which each performer had to provide for herself. The girls chosen had beautiful heads of hair that matched the dresses, not unkempt and neglected as mine was. Footwear also must be neat and becoming. No! altogether it was out of the question that I should take part, no matter how much I longed to do so.

The pageant took place on a day I happened to be at school, so that I had the intense pleasure at least of watching it. A tall, graceful girl stood on something high right in the centre of the group. Her billowy dress was raised each side to represent angels' wings. On her head she wore a wreath of flowers. The other girls, also in white, were seated beneath her, drooping, as if sleeping and tired. The girl in the centre started to sing, and her voice was clear as a bell:

> 'Come children it's bedtime, the angel in white
> Calls the children to her garden, the garden of the night,
> Where the dream trees shake their blossoms on the
>   heads of all the sleepers,
> And the moonbeams shine in pity on the wet cheeks of
>   the weepers,
> Where the sad ones and the glad ones
> All alike in their slumbers,
> Bless the angel of the garden,

Of the garden of the night.
Where the good ones, and the rude ones,
All alike in their slumber,
Bless the angel of the garden,
The garden of night.'

Never shall I forget that lovely scene. It had the comforting and uplifting effect of making me feel that all children were equally dear to somebody or something.

In the early autumn I often went with Pratt on blackberrying excursions. We would rise very early and walk miles, while the early morning mist had to me a beauty all its own. We took large baskets, and somehow Pratt knew just where the spots were that nobody else ever seemed to visit. Some of these isolated and shady spots were shut in and rather creepy, but we were well paid for the trouble of climbing through and over hedges and thorns, for we found and picked the largest and most luscious clusters of berries that I have ever seen in my life. Pratt sold these to the shops and, I believe, he found it very profitable.

My clothes, already torn and ragged for the most part, were not improved by these excursions. I do not think Mrs Pratt worried over such matters, for well she knew the more ragged I looked, the more chance there was that I should bring home a bundle of clothing from some singing expedition.

Autumn gave place to winter. One cold clear day we set out for Sennen Cove, several miles away. As usual we sang before isolated cottages on the way to the cove. It always delighted me as I caught a glimpse of homely interiors when cottage doors were opened by someone bringing out a copper. There would be a flicker of firelight, for these cottage interiors were usually very dark, and plants in the living-room window, while very picturesque, often partially excluded the daylight. One usually saw just inside the door a large chest of drawers upon which stood many family photographs. Sometimes it would be a mahogany round table that held the photographs. Usually also there were artificial flowers under a glass case. The large family Bible would be very prominent too.

Sometimes I was reminded of the cottage at Redruth Church town by what I saw in these interiors: perhaps a fancy box on the table all studded with tiny sea-shells of every description, just like my aunts used to make; or again a horn might rest on the family Bible just as it did in Grandmother's cottage. Whether the horn had any purpose or was just an ornament I don't know. Occasionally, too, one would see coloured woollen frames made in the shape of a star hanging on the walls with a small photograph in the centre. These also used to be made by my aunts. Such things are never seen now, but I often saw them in my singing days and they always stirred up memories of that first dear home.

It seemed that we had been singing at Sennen Cove not very long before lamps began to be lit. The wind began to moan and to cut through one's clothing. I clapped my hands every now and then to bring warmth into them.

The lamplit cottages looked homely and inviting. I imagined families gathered around firesides, laughing, chatting, and a longing would sweep over me to be one of a real family, happy and carefree, decently clothed and clean. How lovely I thought it must be not to be looked down upon by other girls.

The distant lighthouse began to twinkle. This took my mind off myself and my own troubles, for I had heard a story about this same lighthouse and this now occupied my thoughts. As I gazed out to sea at the lighthouse, while tramping towards another group of cottages, waves were mounting higher and higher, dashing on the rocks. I shivered with the cold. Now we were singing:

'Let your lower lights be burning,
Send a gleam across the wave,
Some poor fainting struggling seamen
You may rescue, you may save.'

Doors opened here and there, while somebody would come out hurriedly with a copper. Women who did so would wrap shawls more closely round them and with a hurried kindly word would disappear again into a warm lit room, shutting the doors behind them.

By the time we had worked the whole village it was dark and Pratt decided at last we must turn our steps homeward.

Just then a door opened and a woman came out, carrying a paper parcel. 'Here, my dear,' she said, 'here's a few things might be useful for you.' Without waiting to be thanked she had returned to her little family whom I had seen standing inside the open door. Before the door closed, 'Good night' called half a dozen voices of all ages.

I did not open my parcel until I reached home. As we left the cove, the cutting wind was in our faces. It grew very dark on the lonely country road, though the lights of Penzance miles away in the distance showed a comforting glow against the sky. As we battled against the wind, I thought we should never reach home that night. I was so tired I could have lain in the ditch and slept. Every now and then, however, fresh life seemed to come to me as I remembered the parcel under my arm and I wondered what it would contain. Would it be something pretty? if so should I be allowed to keep it?

Presently a sound behind us frightened me and set my heart thumping. A tree had crashed down where a minute before we had passed. The wind continued to shriek and moan, and Pratt, who had hardly said a word since we left the cove, now spoke: 'I should think seven devils are let loose tonight,' he said.

At last we reached the crossroads. Above the wind we

heard a pony and trap coming from the direction of St Just. The driver, as he drew near to us, stopped the pony.

'Jump in,' he said, 'and be quick. I'm on my way to fetch a doctor. My wife has been taken ill.'

'Well, you might be glad you haven't come on the Sennen Road,' said Pratt, as he took a seat, 'for a tree has just crashed down behind us.'

'The storm is doing quite a lot of damage back at St Just,' said the driver.

I was thankful for the lift, and very soon we had reached the doctor's house, where we parted company with the kindly driver. The streets were more sheltered than the open country, and we soon reached home.

When I opened my parcel there was a tidy serviceable dress in it and a woman's hat. The dress was not a good fit, but I wore it the next day, also did I wear that hat, though it was hopelessly unsuitable for one so young.

The next day was Sunday, and I dressed up in this hat to go to the Church Sunday School. The hat was stylish and on a woman of thirty would have looked very nice I've no doubt; but though I did not realize it at the time, it looked very ridiculous on me. All the same, I fancied myself, and as I entered the church I affected a mincing walk as I had seen well-dressed girls do.

The other pupils sniggered. My teacher, Miss Butler, a small elderly lady of whom I stood in great awe (as she always wore a dark veil and one could never see her face), looked at me reprovingly; at least I thought she did, as far as I could tell through the thickness of her veil. I began to feel hot and uncomfortable all over.

After Sunday School we trooped out of church. The wind was rising again now, and in spite of elastic, I had to hold the hat on. The wretched thing sat like a pimple on the top of my head and the elastic was very loose. I decided I would go for a walk along the sea front, though I was supposed to go straight home after school. The wind rose higher and higher. A couple of girls called after me – 'Where did you get that hat? Oh you lucky beggar.' A sudden awful gust of wind – I didn't get my hand up quick enough, and the next minute there was this wretched hat floating on the sea. Well – it's an ill wind . . .

It was early January, 1906. Everybody, including myself, knew vaguely that my birthday occurred in that month. Nobody however knew the date, or my correct age. 'She is a great big maid,' said Pratt, 'she must be fourteen, and she's to leave school and come with me every day.'

Mrs Pratt looked uneasy. She also would have liked me to leave school and bring more to the family purse. However, she had a greater respect for the law than her husband.

'We had better make sure,' she said.

'Make sure be blowed,' said Pratt. 'She is fourteen if I'm a day.'

I told my teacher I was to leave school because Pratt said I must be fourteen.

The headmistress, who had strong doubts about the matter, set whatever machinery was necessary in motion, with the result that the school authorities demanded a birth certificate. This angered Pratt very much, and I heard a great many remarks from him about great big maids eating their heads off and learning a lot of tripe that was no good to them.

First of all my grandfather had to be contacted, then in due course the certificate arrived. Pratt, much to his disgust, was proved wrong, for this important bit of paper proved beyond a doubt that I should become twelve years old on the twenty-fourth of that month. My headmistress and class teacher were triumphant. They were sure all along that I was much younger than Pratt made out. Moreover they both genuinely liked me and wished to see me get on at school.

Then I fell ill. I had a nasty attack of chicken pox, which on account of the neglected condition of my hair became very serious. Sores broke out all over my head, and when I next put in an appearance at school, I was sent home as not being in a fit state to be with the other children.

This was to me the last straw. I felt now more disgraced and humiliated than ever before. Pratt's continuous nagging, on top of all the mental strain I had borne on his account, now drove me desperate. I could bear no more. I suddenly made up my mind I would run away.

Telling Mrs Pratt I was attending a free breakfast the following morning gave me the excuse for early rising.

The next morning I set out with just the clothes I stood up in, and not one penny in my pocket.

I never saw Mr or Mrs Pratt again.

CHAPTER 9

I Run Away

IT HAD BEEN SNOWING ALL NIGHT. THE SNOW NOW LAY THICK and hard on the ground. Cart tracks made it uneven and difficult for walking. My boots were in a bad state. All these troubles, however, were more than counterbalanced by my new-found freedom. Once more I became Emma Smith.

I planned to walk to Redruth Church town, where I would call at our old home. Vaguely I felt that the very sight of the cottage would somehow end all my troubles.

Where I should find bed and food had not so far troubled me. Just the sight of the old home, I felt, would put everything right. I had left Penzance without having breakfast, and now, after walking for a couple of miles, the pangs of hunger made themselves felt. The question now was how could I get some food so as to be able to continue my journey, which in all would be about seventeen miles. I could always sing, of course, but I was afraid that if I sang alone it would attract the attention of a policeman who would assuredly take me back to Pratt.

I decided that sing I would, but not in the village of Marazion where I now found myself, though at that moment I was quite near a baker's shop. Bread and cakes were displayed temptingly in the window. No! it was too risky. I would try at some wayside cottage further afield.

I left the village behind; it looked very lovely under its mantle of snow, but I had no eye just then for beauty; I was too much concerned with my gnawing appetite. 'Crunch, crunch,' I went over the frozen snow.

I came to a cottage garden gate. I looked furtively round for a possible policeman, but not only was there no policeman in sight, there was nobody else either. Here then I would try my luck. I stood before the door and started to sing 'Safe in the arms of Jesus.' The door opened. A woman with a strained, sorrowful look stopped me at once.

'Don't, my dear, don't sing here,' she said. 'Can't you see my blinds are drawn?'

So intent had I been upon getting food that I had not noticed the windows of the cottage, probably the first thing I should have noticed at any other time. I started to cry, because I was perplexed and sorry about the woman and her trouble, and sorry for myself, and ashamed of myself, too, that I had been so thoughtless.

'Come in, my dear,' she said, 'you didn't mean no harm. I'm just going to have a cup of tea; could you drink one?'

I nodded; I could not speak just then.

The good soul laid her table and placed cups and saucers for two. She made some tea and spread bread and butter. Then she said: 'Come, my dear, draw your chair up. I can see you're cold and famished. Where have you come from?'

Before I could reply she said, looking more closely at me: 'I've seen you before; you came here back along with that little humped-back man that goes round singing.' I admitted I was the same.

'I'm sorry about the blinds,' I said, after I'd done full justice to the meal.

The kind-hearted woman had not touched a morsel herself, though she had laid for two. She was sitting now hunched over the fire, staring at it in dumb misery. I think she had forgotten all about me. The clock on the mantelpiece ticked loudly; it sounded homely.

The woman raised her head and looked at me; her eyes now were full of tears. She said: 'My husband and my only son are both lying dead upstairs. They were all I had got in the world.'

Again she slumped into that hopeless position, just staring, staring into the fire. I was tongue-tied. The awfulness of the woman's sorrow seemed to be something that I could not comment upon. I wanted to get out quick from this house of death, where I felt so ill at ease. The woman had been kind to me, however, and fed me well. I felt I could not rush away; I sat silent.

After what seemed like ages, she spoke again. 'My husband was one of the best,' she said. 'My boy was an idiot, but I loved him all the more because of it. Now they are both gone.'

I still sat silent and ill at ease. There was nothing, nothing that I could say. I wondered vaguely how it had come to pass that both her dear ones should have died at the same time. I could not ask, and she did not say.

After a while I said, 'Please can I go now?' The poor woman roused herself.

'Yes, my dear,' she said, 'and look! Take this bit of bread and butter with you. You'd better hurry up home now, you shouldn't be wandering around like this by yourself.'

I took the paper bag and thankfully escaped. I was terribly sorry for the poor kind woman, but I could not show it. I decided that this bread and butter must now carry me through the rest of my journey. I could not run the risk of running into something awful like that again.

'Goodbye, my dear,' she called after me sadly. I waved farewell. The woman closed her door upon herself and her sorrow.

It was about eleven o'clock when I walked into the little town of Hayle. This I knew was seven miles from Penzance. I had then another ten to go before I would reach the cottage at

Redruth. I found a sheltered spot where I could eat the bread and butter that poor grief-stricken woman had given me. I could not sit down to rest because snow lay thick everywhere. I was thirsty, so I picked up some clean snow and put it into my mouth. Beating my hands together to bring a little warmth into them, I now stepped out again. Milestone succeeded milestone; ten became nine; nine became eight; eight became seven; and so on. Daylight was fading as I entered Camborne. I now had another three miles to go. I should have been in Redruth before this had my footwear been more comfortable, and if the snow had not been so hard and uneven to walk upon. As it was, I was beginning to feel excited as I saw the familiar distant hill and knew that the spot I loved best on earth was just the other side.

A nicely dressed girl about my own age now caught up with me, and as she came level with me, she said, 'You got sore feet?'

The truth was, I hadn't thought much about them. My mind was intent upon reaching my destination. Now for the first time I centred my attention upon my feet. 'Yes,' I said.

'I get sore feet sometimes,' she said. 'Then my Ma puts ointment on. Shall you come home with me and let my Ma put ointment on your feet?'

Well, this was an odd question from a perfect stranger. I didn't think the girl looked quite all there. I hesitated for a minute or so while I considered the matter.

The girl stopped before a door. 'I live in here,' she said. 'Come on.'

The girl's mother was evidently used to her daughter bringing in stray suffering animals of all sorts, human or otherwise. I did not have my feet dressed, but I did get something to eat and drink. I can't remember what I told the woman, but I do remember she looked troubled as she parted with me at the door, as though she wondered if she ought to have done something more about me.

It was about an hour after leaving these good people

that I stood on the doorstep of the cottage where I had once lived with my grandfather, and which I had always held in such affectionate memory. Lamplight shone through the drawn blinds. It looked so snug and homely under its snow-covered roof. Who, I wondered, would open the door? I knocked timidly.

The door opened. A small, bent, elderly woman stood before me.

'Please can I come in,' I asked; then added, 'I used to live here with my grandma.'

The little woman drew me inside and looked earnestly into my face. 'My God!' she exclaimed, 'it's Emma Smith. Don't you know me?' she asked, 'I used to live next door. You used to come in and talk to me when you were little.'

'Mrs Pascoe!' I exclaimed with joy.

'The same,' she said. 'Take off your things and come and sit down, and tell us how you managed to find your way here. And why you are alone,' she now said, as she busied herself with cups and saucers.

For the first time that day I removed my woollen tam-o'-shanter. Mrs Pascoe looked horrified as she saw the state I was in. 'I've had chicken pox,' I said, in miserable explanation.

She poured boiling water into the teapot. 'Chicken pox shouldn't have got you in *that* state,' she said.

As I gazed round the room, I was filled with a mixture of emotions. The dear room that was the same and yet not the same. Grandmother's furniture had gone, but there were one or two things about here and there that I knew had been hers. The mantelshelf contained the same china ornaments, a lady and gentleman each on a horse and facing each other.

Mrs Pascoe followed my eyes. 'Yes, they were your grandmother's. She gave them to me when you all went to Plymouth,' she said.

The furniture the room now contained was vaguely familiar, because I had often run in and out of the next door cottage in the old days when Mrs Pascoe lived there. I felt I wanted to cry, it was all such a mixture. I loved being here in this dear cottage again, but Grandmother was not here. I was happy to have found an old neighbour of whom I had been fond as an infant, and who I knew had been a great friend of my grandmother; but I was ashamed and sorry as I looked into the sweet old face to see she was so worried about me and shocked at my appearance. It was all very bewildering and such a mixture of joy and peace, shame and sorrow. Besides I was desperately tired and footsore. I could bear up no longer.

'Come my dear, don't cry,' Mrs Pascoe said. 'We must see what can be done.'

A tall figure, slightly bent, now stood in the doorway. 'Look Emma, do you remember Mr Pascoe?' his wife said.

I dried my eyes and looked at the grey-haired man who had now sat himself in an armchair, regarding me with a puzzled look.

Mrs Pascoe went up close to her husband and shouted in his ear, 'It's Emma Smith.' She shouted it three times.

Then he said impatiently, 'Well, I can see that, but what's the poor little maid doing here in that state?'

Wearily I told as much of my story as I could, always keeping the worst back. Talking was difficult because the deaf man would insist upon being told all I had said, and when the same sentence was shouted again and again it sounded worse and worse each time.

Presently a smile broke over the old man's face and his eyes twinkled as if he remembered something funny. He stepped outside for a moment, then reappeared carrying a large scythe.

'Remember this Emma?' he said chuckling.

Of course I remembered it. Mr Pascoe was a jobbing gardener and in the old days he used to tease me with this thing, whenever he knew I had been naughty. 'I shall put you in the field and cut you up with the grass,' he used to say. I always believed he would carry out his threat, and I was terrified of that long curved blade. I now laughed through my tears.

'That's better, my dear,' he said.

Mrs Pascoe tied up my head in a handkerchief. 'You'd better lie down on the sofa, Emma, and get some sleep,' she said, 'then we can talk tomorrow, when you feel better.'

The warmth of the room now made my sore scalp irritate beyond endurance. I scratched and scratched my poor head, though I knew I was doing myself a lot of harm. I just could not help myself. Sore, but to a certain extent relieved, I now settled down with a contented sigh. I was at last once again in Grandmother's cottage in Redruth Church town.

I was disappointed the following day to find I was not to be allowed to go out and visit well-remembered spots, such as the churchyard where Grandmother and I used to walk on Sunday afternoons, the Church lane where I had often scampered with our collie dog Shep, the tree around which was a low stone seat where I had played with my little brother. How I longed to visit them all!

'No, Emma, my dear,' Mrs Pascoe said. 'For one thing you need rest, and for another I don't want people to see you in that state. I loved your grandmother and I knew her when she was a girl, for I worked for her mother. Her people were farmers you know. Then we were neighbours and friends for years. No! I don't want anybody to see you like that for her sake. We are going to try and find your grandfather, and if we don't hear in a week, we shall have to go to the police.'

Now there I was for the next few days, instead of enjoying the feeling of being at home as I thought I should, I was quaking inwardly all the time at the thought that the police would come and fetch me and take me back to the Pratts.

Grandfather evidently could not be found, so in due course the police did arrive. I believe there were two of them, but of this I can't be sure. They were kindness itself; I have always liked policemen ever since.

Soon I was saying 'Goodbye' to my old friends. Mrs Pascoe wept as we parted. 'I wished I had heard from your grandfather,' she said.

Shortly I found myself inside Redruth police-station. I have a confused memory of seeing several policemen sitting round on tables drinking tea. I was given tea and biscuits. After this one of the policemen said, 'Come on, Emma, I'm going to take you to the station and put you in the train for Penzance.'

I felt sick with fear. 'You're not going to send me back to Mr and Mrs Pratt, are you?' I asked.

'No, no. You need not be afraid of that. You will be met at. Penzance by another policeman, and he is going to take you to a kind lady,' he replied.

I believe every one of those policemen gave me money. I was never so rich in all my life. I think I must have had nearly a shilling all told.

I left the police station happily as one of the men called after me – 'They're going to make a lady of you, my dear.'

I stepped out of the train at Penzance station and saw a tall good-looking policeman on the platform. I went up to him at once and placed my hand in his. We left the station by the back way that led out to the quay. I began to feel a little uneasy; this way led to the street where the Pratts lived. As we drew near to the bottom of the street I saw one or two children I knew. They stared at me, as I had myself stared before now at drunken men being taken into custody. I held my head high, and as we passed the children I said, 'I'm going to be a lady.' But inwardly I was quaking with fear that the policeman was after all going to turn traitor and lead me to Strawberry Gardens and the Pratts. I heaved a sigh of relief as we passed through into Church Street, then through one or two more streets, until we turned our footsteps into Merton Terrace.

'My Sunday school teacher lives here,' I said.

'I'm taking you to her,' the policeman answered.

My heart beat fast now with fear. I had always stood in great awe of the little black-veiled lady, and now I recalled how often I had heard of girls, 'bad girls', from our street, who had suddenly disappeared. I had never known these young women, but a neighbour would drop in and tell Mrs Pratt about them. A girl would just vanish, then it would be reported that Miss Butler had sent her to a home for bad girls.

'She's not going to send me to a home, is she?' I asked anxiously.

'No, she's going to make you a lady,' he said.

The door of number thirty-one opened in response to our ring. It was opened by a very neat middle-aged servant who herself seemed a grand lady to me. As we stepped into the small hall, Miss Butler herself appeared from her sitting-room. She did not look quite so impressive without her veil.

'Come along, Emma,' she said with dignity.

My friend, the policeman, now took his leave. I longed to run after him. I felt like a bird must feel when it has been put into a cage for the first time.

Soon I was sitting at the table in the small well-kept kitchen, having tea with Miss Butler's servant. She spoke very little to me, and I did not presume to address her.

After tea Miss Butler took me to see a doctor a few doors away. 'This poor child has been ruined by a man,' she said. 'Will you supply me with a certificate?'

The doctor made me remove my tam-o'-shanter. He looked horrified, then said, 'I could not possibly do anything with her in that condition. Shall I write out a plain certificate?'

'No,' Miss Butler said, and we left the surgery.

What this visit to the doctor meant I had not the faintest idea at that time. One word only stuck in my mind with a dreadful significance – 'ruined'. Surely 'ruined' meant that whatever it was that was ruined would never, no never, be of any more use. After all, then, I could never be a lady. Such was my miserable reasoning; all because I did not understand what I had heard.

Later in life, when I recalled that scene, it struck me that that doctor was surely very wrong in that he had been willing to certify something that he knew nothing about.

From the age of six, I had been exposed to moral danger. I had been abused and treated shamefully. Yet, as I became aware years later at an age when I understood these things, I was still in the medical sense of the word a virgin. Yet this doctor, because of his natural fastidious dislike of handling one who was in a neglected and dirty state, had been quite willing to state otherwise. Surely the correct and proper thing to have done was to ask that I might be cleansed and my sores treated, and then to come to his surgery again.

That evening Miss Butler and her servant cut all my hair off, treated my sores, and for the first time for ages I was comfortable and at peace. That is to say as far as my physical state went. Mentally I was in a turmoil. What was to happen to me? Where was I going?

My greatest comfort these next few days was the reading matter with which I was supplied. I remember I read with great interest an allegory called *The Rocky Mountains*, at least I think that was the name. This was, I suppose, the very first book I had read outside the school.

A few evenings later, as I was having a tub in a hip-bath in my bedroom, Miss Butler entered the room carrying a letter. 'I've heard from the Sister Superior of the Home at Bramshot,' she said, 'and she very kindly says she will take you.'

So I was to be sent to a home after all, I thought. So much for the policeman's assurance that I was going to be turned into a lady. I stepped out of the bath and started to dry myself. I wrapped the towel round my face so that Miss Butler should riot see the tears that would come in spite of my trying to keep them back. I could not keep the towel there indefinitely; the rest of me had to be dried.

Miss Butler saw the tears that I was now sucking in through my lips as I sniffed. She was always very dignified. 'You must be very grateful for this chance, Emma,' she said, 'for it is a beautiful home and you will be taught many useful things. Why, some day, you might even be a servant like Selina.' (Selina was the name of her own servant.) Had Miss Butler said that some day I might be a duchess she could not have made it sound more ambitious.

I was dry now and swamped in one of Selina's nightgowns, ready to say my prayers aloud to Miss Butler.

'You must ask God tonight to make you very grateful, Emma,' she said.

'Yes, Miss Butler,' I said, with another sniff.

When safely in bed, I thought over the position. After all, Selina was a lady, I thought. And if I became like her, I should be very grand. Look how she wore that little cap on the top of her head. She made it stick up like that herself, for I had seen her starch and iron it. Then that lovely white embroidered apron with the streamers at the back! She never smiled or talked to me, certainly. But that was, I supposed, because she was so important. One of the few remarks Selina had made to me was that once she herself had been 'rescued' by Miss Butler. I didn't grasp what she had meant, but as I stood almost as much in awe of her as I did of her mistress, I didn't dream of asking. On the whole, then, things might have been worse.

CHAPTER 10

Home in a Penitentiary

I WAS TWELVE YEARS OLD ON THE TWENTY-FOURTH OF JANUARY. Just over three weeks later, that is on the seventeenth of February, I entered a penitentiary. I did not know that it was a penitentiary; even when I did hear the word, it conveyed no meaning.

Miss Butler had dressed me in a long black skirt which she said would be useful for me when I left the home. The waistband had been turned over and over to bring it up short enough for me to walk in. Even so, it touched my boots. I cannot remember what the blouse and jacket were like. I wore my own tam-o'-shanter, which the good but superior Selina had washed and disinfected. Miss Butler placed me in charge of the attendant on the train. I was met at Bramshot station by a young sister. She gasped when she saw me. 'You are very young,' she said, in a reproving tone.

The home was a large rambling ivy-covered house, standing in beautiful grounds. I was taken to the cottage in the grounds to which all newcomers were taken before going over to the house to be interviewed by the Sister Superior. The young novice who had met me at the station now handed me over to the lay sister in charge of the cottage.

'Well!' Sister Mary exclaimed as she looked at me. 'Is

this a nursery now for children?' She addressed nobody in particular, for the novice had disappeared.

A plate of cold beef awaited me on the kitchen table. This was the usual fare for people who had been travelling. I finished my tea, then Sister Mary said, 'Come now and have your bath before I take you over to see Sister Superior.'

I was so clean and spotless these days that I just could not see the sense of yet another bath. 'I've had three already this week,' I said. By this time we were upstairs and my remark had been overheard by a couple of sick girls in the cottage dormitory. They sniggered.

'Hush!' said Sister Mary, reprovingly. 'It is silence-time, girls.'

Soon I was taken through the heavy door which led into a large hall or passage that was beautifully tiled. Sister Mary knocked upon a door.

'Come in,' said a gentle voice.

A very saint-like figure sat in a swivel chair at her desk. She turned round to face us as we entered.

'Please Superior, I've brought Emma,' Sister Mary said.

The Sister Superior drew her veil closely round her, as she regarded me in surprise.

'How old are you, Emma?' she said, after a long pause. 'Twelve, Sister,' I answered.

'How very, *very* sad,' she said gravely.

I could not be expected to follow her thoughts. It seemed to me there must be something uncommonly sad in the fact of being twelve. It was not until long, long afterwards that I realized that it was just taken for granted that I was a young prostitute. Had I not run away from Pratt when I did, I should almost certainly have become such a one in time. It could almost be said, I think, that I had left just in the nick of time. As it was, I was no more a prostitute that Dickens's Oliver Twist was a thief, if I may draw upon a character of fiction to illustrate what I mean. Yet here I was placed in this category, and indirectly it has affected my whole life, as will be seen later on in my story.

The Sister Superior was kindness itself, but I understood little of what she was saying. The gist of it all was to the effect that I was never on any account to talk of my past life, that I must keep the rules of the house, and so on. If she asked me (as I believe she did) whether I understood what she was saying, I nervously said, 'Yes, Sister.' She rose and, drawing her veil more closely still around her, said, 'Come, Emma, I will take you to the classroom.'

The Sister Superior opened a door of a room from which a babel of voices could be heard. There was an instant silence as she entered. On a dais in the corner sat the novice who had met me at the station. Her black outdoor veil had been replaced by the white veil of her novitiate. This held my attention.

'I have brought Emma to you,' the Sister Superior said, addressing the novice. Turning to the rest of the room, she spoke again. 'Emma is rather young, so you will all be very kind to her and set her a good example, won't you?'

'Yes, Sister,' replied a chorus of voices.

The head classroom girl now came forward and showed me to the one empty chair which was now to be my seat. The Sister Superior withdrew from the room, as one of the girls held the door open for her. The girl curtsied as she sailed out, her veil clutched tightly around her. Instantly bedlam broke loose again. 'Oh, what a shame!' seemed to be the one cry that broke from about twenty voices. Bewildered by the noise and the sea of faces around me, I asked innocently, 'What's a shame?' Nobody enlightened me. 'What,' I demanded to know (as I pointed to the novice in charge), 'what has she got that white thing on for?' A roar of laughter greeted this innocent question, and I was more bewildered than ever. These people were funny.

Now everybody seemed to ask me at once, 'How old are you, Emma?' I was getting tired of answering this question, but once again I repeated, 'Twelve!' Again those cries of 'Shame!' went up. I gave it up. There seemed no sense to anything.

The novice now rang the bell. 'A little less noise, if you please, girls,' she said, 'or I shall put you into silence.'

My room-companions ranged in ages from about eighteen to forty. Most of them were in their twenties, however.

I had been put into a cotton dress miles too large for me, but I was told a new dress would be made for me later, and, anyhow, Sister Mary had said, 'You will grow.' A cap, tied under the chin, covered my cropped head, which by this time had healed. A blue and white check apron covered the front of the dress. I certainly looked pretty queer, but at least I was clean and tidy. Black thick woollen stockings that had been lumpily darned again and again, and black heavy boots (the right size at least) completed my outfit. We were all dressed alike, except that the girls who were in their second year boasted a little lace around the hem of their caps. But it was some time before I was able to sort all this out.

One by one the girls obtained permission to leave their seats and brought over small gifts to me. I had started to weep at the strangeness of everybody and everything. 'Dinna greet,' said a kindly Scottish voice. The speaker offered me a small bag of lavender and invited me to sniff. I had been given a large clean white handkerchief. I now dabbed my eyes and obediently sniffed. It was good and reminded me of the cottage gardens. Another girl brought me a hand-made pincushion full of gaily coloured pins she had made herself, and which she called 'points'. 'I'll teach you to make them,' she said. Another brought me some perforated cardboard and silks. 'I'll teach you to work texts,' this girl said. So it went on. Soon I had collected quite a store of treasures. Then the classroom girl (corresponding to a monitress at school) produced a wooden box in which I could keep all my gifts. The novice in charge now rang the five-minute bell which produced silence, and each girl placed the wooden box containing her individual possessions, and which she called her recreation, into the large cupboard provided for the purpose.

The supper-bell rang. Everyone took her place in a long line at the foot of which I was placed. Supper consisted of a light meal of pudding and a mug of badly made cocoa. The meal was at eight o'clock, after which the girls returned to their classrooms until the service of compline which took place at nine.

I was not allowed to stay up for compline, and at 8.30 one of the senior girls was ordered to show me to bed. I was shown into a very long dormitory with several dormer windows. There were about eighteen beds in the room. One candle burned at the far end of the room, throwing deep shadows everywhere, which, when the senior girl had left me, I found rather creepy. I undressed and knelt to say my prayers aloud as I had done at Miss Butler's house. I was about half-way through the Lord's Prayer when my blood froze as a hand was placed on my shoulder. The long shadowy room was, I thought, empty.

I could not bring myself to open my eyes until a voice whispered in my ear, 'We don't say our prayers aloud here.'

The voice was human, so plucking up courage I opened my eyes to see who the voice and hand belonged to, for I had heard no footstep. A girl of about twenty-two stood beside me in her white nightgown and streaming long hair. She returned to her bed in a dark corner of the room. She had been suffering from a bad cold and had been in bed all day. I had not noticed any bed occupied as I had entered. I wonder I had not screamed the place down, I was so frightened at that sudden grip on my shoulder.

I was still awake when about sixteen more people entered. They all undressed in dead silence, brushed their hair, knelt in silent prayer by their bedsides, then got into bed. A little peephole in the wall opened and the sister sitting in the adjoining room, having satisfied herself that all was well in the dormitory, now came in and blew out the candle.

I turned in bed to face the largest window. There was my old friend the moon playing hide and seek among the clouds. A curious sense of comfort stole over me. In all this strangeness, this was something I knew and had loved all my life. Snores were already coming from one or two beds. This strange day had at last come to an end and now I slept.

I was awakened the following morning by the ringing of a large bell that had been brought right into the room. Most of the girls rose at once. They made a bee-line for the tin washbasins at the end of the room. Ice that had formed in the night on the top of the water-can had to be somehow broken before water could be poured into the basins.

I watched and imitated the dressing procedure, which was done as decently as possible under the circumstances. All garments were put on before the nightdress came off. That is, except the dress. This took a little practice to do gracefully.

After dressing, beds were carefully stripped, the bedding laid over the chair. A bell rang. We all lined up outside our dormitory, and the class sister now led us down to the dining-hall. This was lit by a couple of lamps hanging on nails on the wall. Behind the globe there was a round reflector, which helped to give a brighter light.

We were supplied with mugs of tea from an urn, after grace was said. There were plates of dry bread provided, and at the head of one table the class sister served out dripping or treacle, whichever the individual girl preferred. This breakfast never varied throughout the year, except on high festivals when butter took the place of dripping.

The food throughout was not in the same class as that supplied at the Salvation Army Home where I had spent some months about three years before. I just state this as a fact, not as a complaint, for it did not affect me in any way. I was young, with a healthy appetite, and whatever was placed before me, I ate heartily.

After breakfast, we returned to the classroom, where each girl in turn repeated aloud a collect or some portion of scripture that she had had to learn by heart. This was usually preceded by the singing of a morning hymn, and followed by spiritual teaching from one of the sisters.

At eight o'clock a bell rang, and the work of the day started, though for several hours before this, early morning workers had been at their various tasks.

The Home consisted of three groups of girls. Those who lived and worked in the needlework department – this also included housework. Then there were about thirty girls in the laundry. Finally there were six or eight girls employed in the kitchens.

I had, in the beginning, been placed in the needlework department. Beautiful work was turned out here. In those days the Home specialized in the making of trousseaux and layettes. Some girls, especially if in anyway disabled, sat sewing all day. Others had housework to do; when they had satisfactorily finished it, they would then come to the needlework room and take up whatever sewing they had in hand. The most beautiful children's smocks used to be made from time to time, and I have always regretted that I did not learn this lovely art when I had the chance; but at the time that I was a member of that class, I found it extremely difficult to sit for so many hours at a time, or to concentrate on the work in hand. This, I think, could only be expected from one so young.

For a little while I sat all day at my seam or hem, or whatever had been allotted to my task. Precious little sewing did I do, but that little was by way of training. For the most part, I must have been a real headache to the sister or visitor who happened to be sitting on the dais in charge. For I could not keep my seat; if I was told to sit down once during the day, I suppose I must have been told fifty times at least.

The hour of the day I dreaded most was the half-an-hour following tea, when we all had to stand until our work

110

was examined. I was always ashamed of the smallness of the amount I had got through during the day, and was very ill at ease when sister came round to me with spectacles on the tip of her nose. I do not remember that I was scolded unduly, however.

The one bright spot in the day in this class, and what I missed terribly when moved to another, was the hour between three and four in the afternoon when a story book would be read aloud by whoever was in charge. Many a time the reader would look up from her book and catch me with both elbows resting on the table, chin cupped in both hands, while my needlework had slipped to the floor. Then, when I was told to get on with my work, there would be a frantic search for my needle which invariably seemed to have disappeared in the crack of the floorboards.

After a while, it was decided that I needed more exercise, so I was given some housework to do in the mornings under supervision. I did not find the same patience in those whose task it was to train me, as I had found in my teachers at school.

Then they tried me in the laundry. Now I had too much exercise, and by the end of a working-day I was standing first on one leg, then on another, trying to rest each in turn. On washing-days I would be soaked through and through, from neck to feet, for the tubs were high (at least to me). Water trickled all down from my hands to my armpits, from my so-called water-proof apron down to and in my boots. 'Squelch! Squelch!' went my boots as I walked up to the dining-hall.

Later still, somebody had a bright idea that the kitchen might be the best place for me. So into the kitchen I went. I started from the bottom: this was pots and pans. Oh, those great iron saucepans! The things were always burnt. My sink was about six feet long and three feet wide; this would be piled with sticky burnt saucepans and tins. It seemed I could never get through them. It was my job to scrub the potatoes

111

that had to be steamed in their jackets – potatoes for about seventy people. I used to put them in a bath and, as water poured on them, I scrubbed them with a yard broom; then a wheel had to be turned which poured water in the tank. All the kitchen staff took it in turns to do this. What a feast it was for sore eyes when at last my sink was clear for the day and my large scullery clean and tidy!

One duty I had to perform, which was a mixture of pleasure and pain; this was on Saturday mornings. I had to rise at three in the morning to help the cook clean the huge kitchen stove. The painful part was the rising at such an hour when I was dead sleepy, also the uncurtained kitchen windows would make me feel very nervous. For, once, when the cook happened to be absent for a few minutes, I happened to glance round nervously with my blacklead brush suspended in mid-air, when a white face appeared at a window, or it seemed white, framed as it was with the darkness of night around it. I screamed with fright, which caused me to be punished, for from the hour of compline to the hour after Mass was celebrated the following morning, dead silence all through the house was strictly observed. A scream soon after 3 a.m. was an unpardonable crime. It turned out to have been a policeman on his rounds, and seeing the kitchen lighted at this early hour, he had looked through the window to investigate. This episode left me very nervous lest I might so disgrace myself again.

The pleasurable part of it was that when the stove was all bright and shining and the kettle boiling, the cook would make a cup of tea which we would sit and drink with a slice of the sisters' 'hardbake'. This was a cross between cake and pudding and was eaten in the refectory at supper-time. The girls also had hardbake for supper; but the sisters' hardbake was much nicer than ours, hence the sense of privilege in having tea and 'sisters' hardbake'.

Each of the girls in the Home had a teacher, or, should I say, each sister had a number of pupils. Half an hour a week would be allotted as a rule to each pupil. The girls for the most part became attached to their teachers and looked forward to that weekly half an hour. The pupil would learn the whole, or part, of a chapter of the New Testament that had been set for her the previous week, or in some cases it was a catechism that had to be learnt by heart. Then teacher or pupil would read aloud from some religious book, after which a little discussion took place.

I became devoted to my teacher. Sister Helen was a middle-aged lady of sweet and gentle ways. She had been away in retreat when I first entered the Home and had returned a week later. Almost from the first time she had spoken to me, I gave her my heart. All my yearning for affection and for somebody upon whom I could bestow affection, was now centred upon Sister Helen. Not only was I attached to her person, but even her bed-sitting-room, her books, her plants, in fact anything that could be said to belong to Sister Helen was loved by me.

If I was deeply attached to my own particular teacher, the reverse was the case in regard to my kitchen class sister. I heartily disliked her, and could do nothing right for her. She expected as much work from me, performed at the same speed, as would be expected of a woman of thirty. I can hardly ever recall a smile or a kind word from her, while my punishments were many and severe.

This sister even locked me in a little cell alone the whole of one night for some trivial offence. I was only thirteen at the time; it does not soften the memory when I recall that I was taken ill in the night. I think my crime had been that I had bumped into her sacred person when running round a corner of a long passage. I had burst into uncontrollable laughter at the time; I had been rushing like a mad thing, when I should have walked sedately and, as I drew near to her, I should have respectfully curtsied.

The religious work that I would be called up to read aloud to Sister Helen was always far above my head. I would

follow the lines with my finger on each word, and when I
came to the hard words, all I could do was to spell them out.
No sense of the meaning of anything I read ever penetrated
my brain. But it was enough that I was sitting in the same
room as my beloved teacher. What, in my opinion, did the
silly old book matter? If the religious works were difficult
and impossible for me to understand, this was offset by the
ordinary library books that we were always allowed to read at
meals. The meals were silent, except for Sunday tea-time; and
at Christmas, Easter and Whitsun, we were allowed to talk
at dinner-time.

The food was not always as good and as plentiful as
it might have been, but with a good library book to look
forward to, meal times were certainly a pleasure. Our books
were changed once a week, on Sunday after choral Mass, and
dull indeed was the dinner or tea-time on Friday or Saturday
if one had finished one's book and had to wait for Sunday to
change it. On the other hand, sometimes one had a few pages
more to get through when the week-end came, in which case
one had to read the end and leave out one or two previous
chapters. I owe more than I can say to this privilege in reading
matters.

My favourite stories always were books that were written
about some poor child; perhaps he or she was stolen by gipsies
or merely lost. In the course of time all would come right, the
child would be restored to its doting parents, become well-
dressed and live happily ever after. The first book I ever read
at Bramshot was called *The Bishop's Little Daughter* and was
such a story. I just lived from one mealtime to another to get
at my precious book. I believe at the back of my mind I had
the feeling that perhaps some day I, too, would be discovered
to be a Princess or some such, and that wicked fairies had
changed me at birth. Then I would remember my physical
likeness to my mother and be depressed that nothing exciting
could possibly happen to me.

I do not remember that our library contained one book

of Charles Dickens, so I did not get the chance to read this great man's works until years later.

We were only allowed to write letters once in two months, exceptions being made in the case of girls who had stamped envelopes sent to them. I therefore got very little practice in the art of writing. If my handwriting could only match my reading ability, I should be happy. Even pencils were forbidden. Strange to say Bibles were not allowed in our possession, only the New Testament. This fact filled me with an unhealthy curiosity, and when I had been doing housework and had occasions to dust a Sister's room, if I saw a Bible handy I could not resist having a peep inside to see what was wicked about it. For my only knowledge of the Old Testament had been the beautiful old stories of Samuel, Joseph, Cain and Abel, Moses, Abraham, Daniel and the like. I could *not* imagine what was bad about the old book. When I had opened the Bible with the guilty feeling that I was doing wrong, I would meet one of my old friends, Samuel, Joseph or Daniel, and once again become engrossed in the story. Then the door would open, and whoever was in charge of me would catch me with that open Bible, and I was scolded as if I had been caught doing something shameful.

For all my sordid upbringing, I was, I realize it now, much younger in mind than most girls of my age. I recall that my own daughters at the same age, who had had a normal upbringing, were much more sensible and advanced than I was.

At breakfast time, we each had a book on spiritual matters to read. Breakfast was not an exciting meal.

The convent penitentiary was situated in beautiful surrounding countryside. Twice weekly walks were taken. Our outdoor uniform consisted of a grey shawl and a striped cotton bonnet which we wore over our indoor caps. If, unfortunately, we were caught in a deluge of rain, we simply lifted the skirt of our dresses and pulled it over our hoods and caps and ran along in our navy petticoats. This did not happen very often. In the spring we gathered primroses and other wild flowers on these rambles; in the autumn we gathered blackberries for jam. Simple pleasures these, but they have left pleasant memories behind.

'Emma,' said my teacher one day, 'have you been baptized?'

'I don't know, Sister,' I replied.

'Well,' she said, 'you had better be conditionally baptized. And now you had better prepare for your life-confession which you must make before the conditional baptism.'

Oh, what an ordeal that was. I was given a devotional book with questions for self-examination. I waded through them all. It seemed to me I had broken every commandment and was guilty of everything under the sun.

As I have mentioned elsewhere, it was strictly forbidden to talk of one's past life, so that to no one had I ever confided about Pratt or my singing expeditions. Now that the time had arrived for me to make my first confession, I was weighed down with all these sordid memories. I was innocent of any sin. I was sinned against, but at that age I could not sort it all out. So I went to the confessional, and still I held my tongue about the biggest worry of all. I still did not know how to explain what had happened. The fact that I was never questioned about my past life by my teacher, made it impossible for me to take her into my confidence and ask her help. I was burdened the whole time now with an awful sense of guilt which made me feel older than my years.

For years after this I was never really happy, for, though in private prayer I was sincere and earnest, I always felt that I was in reality a hypocrite in that my confession had not been made in full. I went to confession after this at stated intervals, but it was always the same. I was thirteen years old when I was confirmed. Even about my confirmation I laboured under a sense of being hypocritical; yet I was really very much in earnest about the whole thing, and I could not have been more sincere in my private prayers. But my confession before the chaplain was like a nagging tooth that nothing would ease. It was not until I was sixteen years of age that I confided in full in our chaplain, after which I enjoyed mental peace. Those four years of strain and unhappiness at an age when I had a right to be happy and carefree could never be replaced.

It was about my thirteenth birthday that I had to be removed to the Cottage, ill with bronchitis. I was placed in a cheerful room in which there was another occupant. A young woman, whom I shall call Annie, lay ill in the bed opposite to mine. She had been suffering from a heart attack, and in a day or so was better again, and was able to get out of bed to chat to me. I was struck with her cultured voice and charm of manner. Then I remembered having heard something of her story; or, it would be more correct to say, overheard something of her story. All my life I had found it entertaining to listen to the conversations of my elders, and I recalled that when Annie had been very gravely ill some time previously, I heard the lay sisters discussing her sad case.

The girl came of rich parentage; she showed me a family photograph. There was father and mother, herself and her twin brother, and some other brothers and sisters. In the foreground there was a groom, standing in smart uniform. Annie looked sad as she showed me the picture. Then she picked up some flannelette needlework she had been doing and said, 'I must get on with this, for I shall be going to service soon.'

This girl who had just shown me a picture of her father's rich house and household was quite reconciled to the thought that she must henceforth earn her living in service. She did not complain, but there was a world of sadness in her eyes.

I recalled the conversation I had heard between the Sisters. It went like this:

'Poor dear Annie, so cruel of her people to cast her off like that.'

'Yes, and they won't do a thing for her, not even pay or help pay doctor's fees.'

'Her father says she has made her bed and must lie on it. In fact her name is never mentioned in the home.'

'Well – it's a comfort to know that her twin brother is loyal to her and comes to see her occasionally.'

'Yes, I think he is paying for her little one to be brought up.'

'Apart from the fact of Annie's birth and upbringing, the girl is not strong enough to get her living; she is always having these bad turns.'

So the conversation had proceeded. Now here before me was the subject of their talk. Young I might be, but not too young to feel a deep sympathy for this sorely punished young woman.

Annie laid the photograph down as a lay sister entered the room. Her eyes were red with weeping; in her hand she held some choice black grapes. Approaching my bed she said sadly, 'Emma, Sister Superior says I am to bring you these grapes. They were Sister Martha's; she has passed away.' As she placed the grapes by my bedside, Sister Mary broke down again and hurriedly left the room.

I had seen Sister Martha only once. She was the retired Sister Superior, a German lady. And once, when Sister Helen had been away for her summer rest, I had been sent to her for instruction. I had been in the convent six months then.

As I had entered her room, the old sister had looked shocked, and exclaimed in broken English, 'My dear child! How old are you?'

'Twelve, Sister,' I said with my heart beating fast, for by now I had realized there was something disgraceful in the admission.

'Twelve!' she repeated after me, sinking back into her chair with horror, as if she was thinking, 'What is the convent coming to? Such things were never done in *my* day. You must leave at *once*,' she said, angrily. 'We must send you to a children's home.'

However, the German sister did not get her way, and I heard no more about the matter. That was the only time I had seen the ex-Sister Superior, and now she was dead.

Annie had met her more often and had reason to mourn her passing; she, too, was overcome.

I felt awkward and didn't know what to say, so I turned my attention to those luscious black grapes. Never in all my life had I tasted black grapes before. Sister Mary popped in again and said, 'Oh, Annie, I forgot to say, will you see that Emma does not swallow the pips?'

A few days later I was well enough to stand by Annie at the window and watch the funeral procession. The coffin was borne on the shoulders of village tradesmen, who had known Sister Martha for many years, and she was held in great respect. Then there came her fellow sisters, then lay sisters, then finally a long line of penitents. The chaplain preceded the procession to the nearby cemetery.

Annie looked very sad for the rest of the day. She sat by the bedroom fire working at her flannelette garments; every now and then her needle became idle as she gazed sadly into the fire.

Only three weeks later, I myself was in another long, winding funeral procession. This time the chief mourner that followed the coffin was Annie's twin brother, for this dear, sweet girl was now at rest. Everyone of us followed that sad young man and gave a last look into her grave. No other member of her family was present.

Annie may have disgraced her family by her sin, but she is one of those people whom I have always felt it was a privilege to have met.

CHAPTER 11

Life in a Convent

SOME TIME AFTER MY ILLNESS, I WAS ONCE AGAIN PLACED IN the laundry, and though I still found a long day's work very hard, I did manage it better than before.

The laundry was, for the most part, a cheerful place. Some hours were spent in silence, when more work would be done. Some hours we were allowed to talk or sing. We usually got through the customers' work by Friday afternoon; or if it was holiday season, by the evening. Saturday morning was spent in doing the home washing. After dinner we went for a walk if fine, if wet we sat in our classroom doing our own recreation work, whatever it happened to be. One of our handicrafts was the cutting out of beautiful lace cards.

We purchased (or got a lady visitor to purchase for us) a sheet of perforated cardboard; it was made in Germany, and one never sees it now. We would lay the cardboard on a piece of glass and with a penknife snip out bits here and there until we had made our pattern. In the centre of the card we would place a sacred picture, and if the cut-out pattern was a very elaborate one, we would thread blue or pink ribbon through it.

Some of the girls turned out much more beautiful specimens than I ever managed. Sometimes we used this cardboard for making bookmarker texts, working the words in silks, then stitching them on ribbon. These would make little token gifts for anyone to whom we were attached.

Crochet work was a great favourite pastime in those days, and much beautiful work in that line I have seen performed. Here again, I did not excel.

On Sundays we went to choral Mass at nine-thirty. Our chaplain had a very good voice himself and he would hold singing practice on Saturday evenings for the following day; the result was very good singing indeed.

As I have said before, we changed our library books after this service, and those girls who were due to write a letter were given paper and pen. Letters were not allowed to be sealed down, as they had to be read before posting. In the same way, all letters received were read before being handed over to the owners.

Sunday was a pleasant day spent in pleasant surroundings, for our classroom was light and airy. Two or three sacred pictures adorned the distempered walls, a large crucifix hung over the mantelshelf, and on one wall between two large windows stood the figure of the Madonna and Child. A large stained table stood in the centre of the room, around which were placed as many chairs as could be fixed underneath it. Each of these chairs was the home of one girl. Narrow tables went the length of the room on each side; chairs were placed between these and the wall: again each chair belonged to somebody. Only on high festivals were we allowed to change our seats. The large recreation cupboard stood by the wall opposite the fireplace. In winter we had a coke and cinder fire; the girls who sat near were the luckiest, for they got all the warmth.

In summer, bluebells or picturesque leaves adorned the fireplace. The charge-table stood on a dais in one corner of the room. On this stood the little bell which was used to call the girls to attention for various reasons. A bowl of primroses, or other seasonable flowers, also stood on the charge-table;

and there were always fresh flowers beneath the crucifix and the Madonna.

The windows looked out on to a beautiful part of the garden. We were never allowed to enter the garden, but we did have the pleasure of seeing the flowers that grew therein, and of watching a beautiful magnolia tree bursting into bloom in its appropriate season.

About twenty-five per cent of our girls were of Scottish birth, and many a sweet Scottish song have I heard sung by these girls in the recreation hour: 'Huntingtower', 'Will ye no' come back again', 'By yon Bonny Banks', and the like. The Irish girls, of whom we had a few, also sang lovely old songs pertaining to their country. 'Killarney' was one of these. The English girls were not outdone, and many were the sweet songs I learned by heart after hearing them sung often by these girls. I can only remember one Welsh girl and, true to type, she had a lovely voice. It was good to hear her sing 'My Mother's Sweet Home is in Wales'.

Songs in questionable taste were not only frowned upon, but strictly forbidden, so that one only stored up memories of that which was lovely in this direction.

We had song books called *Old Songs for Young Voices*, and many of these ditties came in useful in after life to sing to my own young children. Some time ago I bought some old gramophone records, among them 'The Mistletoe Bough'. Great was my disappointment when I played it. Could this possibly be the same song, I wondered, that we used to sing, and through the singing of which I lived through all the different emotions of the poor bridegroom? I shared the bridegroom's loneliness and anxiety, as he searched in vain for his missing bride, and cold shivers of horror ran down my spine as, with him (now an old man), I stood by the open chest and saw the skeleton of the bride, with the bridal wreath still on her brow. And when, one day, one of the sisters assured us solemnly that her mother had seen this very chest, it was all doubly real.

I wonder if my own children ever get the pleasure from wireless and gramophone that we used to get from singing together, or listening to each other singing, these old songs. I wonder!

Christmas-time always brings back affectionate memories of the Home at Bramshot. First there would be the learning and practising of carols; this I always loved. On the walk we took nearest the day itself, we would bring in armfuls of evergreens and holly. Mistletoe was never used. Then on Christmas Eve one of the lay Sisters would decorate our classroom and erect the crib. That evening we went a little earlier than usual to bed, and were called again at eleven o'clock, when we rose, tired and shivering, and a bell would summon us to our own classrooms where a cup of cocoa was given us to drink before we entered the chapel for the midnight Mass. In my imagination, I really was about to enter Bethlehem.

As we took our places in chapel, still feeling shivery but excited, the first thing one saw was the beautiful Crib on the altar step. The chapel was beautifully decorated. Then the organ would peal forth the first notes of that old carol that I have never heard anywhere else – 'Let us now go to Bethlehem'. For weeks past we had been practising it until we had got the Latin words of the chorus perfect.

No Christmas nowadays ever gives me the thrill that those Christmases used to give me.

The following day, letters and parcels would be given out; that to me was the one sad hour, for never a parcel came my way. I think I was almost without exception the only girl not to receive a Christmas parcel from somebody, and when you realize that I was years younger than any of the others, it will be readily understood that I found it hard to bear.

However, these girls were for the most part extremely generous and shared whatever they had received with those less fortunate. You readers who buy your sweets each week can have no idea what a luxury a chocolate from one girl, an orange from another, a slice of cake from yet another, and on top of that a few nuts or dates from yet another parcel-receiver could be.

At dinner on Christmas day we were allowed to talk. This was more of a treat to the non-bookworm than it was to a lover of books such as myself. All the same it lent a festive air to the occasion. Dinner consisted of roast pork and Christmas pudding, into which some silver threepenny pieces had been placed. I remember I found a threepenny piece on my first Christmas day, and great excitement it caused me.

If it was fine we went for a walk in the afternoon. At tea, a slice of fruit cake was provided. This only happened about three times a year, so even that helped to make the festival.

Instead of keeping Boxing day, we kept the following Saturday as Tree day. The whole day was a holiday except for urgent duties. In the evening we all trooped into the dining hall, where a huge Christmas tree stood in the centre of the room. It was lit with candles, and one of the younger sisters stood nearby with a snuffer on a long handle in case of accidents.

Everybody in the house assembled in the room, also the gardener and his wife, and the laundryman and his family.

The chaplain gave out the presents; a large and small present for everyone. The large present would, in a girl's first year, consist of a work-box set up with cottons, etc.; the second year girls received some calico or flannelette to make herself some garment that would be useful when she went out to service. The small present might be a little china shoe or fancy box or something of the sort. I think laundry customers were usually the donors of these.

Carols were sung. The chaplain, who had a sense of humour, would make some funny remarks as he handed the presents round, and a good time was had by all.

*   *   *

Though the penitents were not allowed the use of the gardens in front of the house, we had our own little patches of garden in the recreation grounds, and prizes were given for the best show of the year. Two years was the usual time each girl stayed in the Home, but there were exceptions. Occasionally a girl would be frightened of facing the world again and would stay on indefinitely and become a useful member of the household. As time went on I learned to love the Home dearly; every stick and stone of the place became dear to me. I did not realize how dear, until for a while I left it.

While it is true that those incomplete confessions of mine weighed on my conscience to such a degree that I could never really be lighthearted and happy as a girl of my age should be, this did not prevent me from being devoted to the place, and to a few people in it; Sister Helen being my first and greatest love.

I was about thirteen and a half when one summer afternoon I was informed that the Sister Superior wished to see me. I always stood a little in awe of this lady; her habit of drawing her veil around her as she gazed solemnly at me, I found rather alarming.

I often found myself in trouble over silly trifles, such as once when a novice reported me for giggling in chapel. I have always had a sense of humour, and sometimes another girl, knowing this, would whisper something funny to me while in evensong or compline. And I have once or twice been called to the Superior's room for a scolding; on one occasion she threatened to send me to a reformatory. I don't think she could really have meant it, for surely one does not go to a reformatory for giggling in church; but at the age I was then, one always believed in a threat.

Many years later, when I had learned to love this good sister, I confided to her my early fear of her. She was, I think, hurt and sorry when I told her.

When the message came on this summer's afternoon, I searched my conscience for possible misdemeanours, but for once I could not think of anything. So trying not to feel too nervous, I straightened the bow under my chin, smoothed my apron, blew my nose, cleared my throat and walked sedately to the Sister Superior's room. At least I was on my way there when I saw a sight that made me stop dead in my tracks. Sitting on a window-ledge in the front hall and opposite the Sister Superior's door was the familiar beloved figure of my blind grandfather. Beside him stood a boy of about eleven, whom I knew at once must be Harry.

Forgetting completely that silence was the order in passages and corridors, I made one bound and with the glad cry of 'Grandad', I was hugging that dear man as childishly as I had done at Penzance fair-ground about three years before. Harry and I laughed shyly at each other. Then the Sister Superior, who had opened her door and was kindly smiling at us all, now told me to take Grandfather and Harry over to the Cottage, where we could all have tea.

The good lady accompanied us to the cottage door, still drawing that veil tightly round her; but in place of her usual grave expression, her face now wore an indulgent smile. Sister Superior handed us over to the care of Sister Mary, who had already laid tea for three in the visitors' room.

I asked Grandfather how he had found out my whereabouts. It appears he had made many enquiries, and at last found out the truth, when he lost no time in making this journey (with the help of Harry) to visit me. He told me that my mother had had two more children since I had last seen her. I am afraid I was not very much interested in this family news, for I had hardly given my mother a thought since we parted a few years before in Mrs Pratt's tenement room at Plymouth. In the circumstances this was hardly surprising.

Harry said, 'Emma looks like a lady, Granda.'

'You've grown a lot,' said Grandfather, stretching out his hand in the old familiar way and placing it on my head.

'Who's looking after you now?' I asked.

'Oh, I'm married again, and she's a good woman,' said the old man proudly.

Somehow I felt a pang of jealousy on my dear grandmother's account; yet at the same time I was glad to think he was well looked after, as he certainly appeared to be.

The door opened, and my laundry class sister came in. She chatted for a little while, and presently she asked, 'How many children did you have, Mr Smith?'

Grandfather turned his head in the speaker's direction. 'Twenty-three, born and christened,' he answered simply.

'Twenty-three!' echoed Sister Gertrude horrified. 'And you a blind man,' she added reproachfully.

Grandfather's face wore a puzzled look as though he couldn't work that one out. Or perhaps the presence of Harry and myself prevented any reply he might otherwise have made.

Sister Gertrude then said, 'Come, Emma, I'm afraid you must get back to the house now.'

I hugged Grandfather again, and gave Harry a sisterly kiss, and we parted.

After this event I was able to look forward to an occasional letter, for Grandfather got somebody to write for him now and then, and great was my excitement when the letter was handed to me. I should have been still more thrilled had I had the privilege of opening the letter myself.

Somewhere about this time I was very much upset at the departure of Sister Helen for work in another Home; so devoted had I become to her that I could not imagine life going on without her.

Some people were cruel enough to say that I should do better without her for she spoilt me. They were, I think, wrong. What these people meant by 'spoiling' was that sometimes Sister Helen was a little indulgent towards me in a way that she was not to her other pupils. It was, I think, that she remembered my age and, when possible, treated me accordingly.

Once when I had been disgraced by being put down to the very bottom of my class, that is I took my place in the dining hall and elsewhere below the very last new girls – all because I would talk in the dormitory – it was Sister Helen who, instead of showing displeasure (as I suppose she ought to have done), requested instead that I should be allowed to go out on to the lawn and pick marguerites for a lady visitor. This privilege did far more to help me than the punishment had done, which I think shows that Sister Helen understood her pupil more than my class sister did. And now she was leaving us, and I felt that the world would never be the same.

'I will write to you, Emma,' my teacher promised, as we had our parting interview. She was as good as her word.

Now I had two correspondents. Somehow the world did go on after Sister Helen's departure, and in time the ache of missing her became less bad.

Was I really fickle, I wonder, in that I became equally devoted to another sister who came to us when I was fourteen; and though I grieved when, through Sister Helen's death, her letters stopped, Sister Kate was for years my whole world.

By this time, although it could not be said that I was a skilled laundress, I was, considering my age, getting on quite well at this work. Our laundry was at that time entirely run by hand.

There was a large ironing room containing several long trestle tables. It was light and airy, having plenty of windows. There was a sorting room and a packing room, and a mangle room that contained an old-fashioned box mangle that was full of stones. At least that's what I was told: one never saw the stones. This was turned by a wheel by one girl, while another would skilfully fill up the rollers that had to be placed in a certain position under the box. This type of mangle pressed sheets, etc., far better than any modern mangle does.

The wash-house was also light and airy with two rows

of washing tubs down the length of the building. One side of the wash-house contained two very large coppers: one for clean hot water, the other for boiling clothes in. A flight of stone steps led up to the coppers. There was a space between the two just large enough to stand.

One day, when washing and boiling was in full swing, the girl whose business it was to see to the coppers was standing on this space with the long copper pole in her hand, and being in a frivolous mood she was playing about. The copper, in which the white clothes were boiled, happened to be boiling at that time. The girl was warned that she must behave more steadily or there might be an accident. Suddenly shrieks rent the air, and poor Isabella had slipped right into that boiling mass.

I am thankful to say I did not witness the appalling accident. The girl was about and well again when I saw her. She then showed me the marks of her ribbed stocking all over her legs which she will bear all her life, for she had been almost up to her waist in that cauldron.

For many weeks Isabella lay in pain at the Cottage, with a cradle over her poor legs. The Bishop of the diocese confirmed her while still in bed.

Some time later, these coppers were removed and more safety measures were taken.

When I first entered the Home, the only means of lighting after dark was by candle-light, in the laundry as elsewhere. Looking back, I can't help thinking it must have been extremely difficult to work well in the flickering lights of a candle here and there. It seemed like fairyland when we changed to oil lamps; yet that also would have seemed dim to us after we had changed to electric light. But these changes took a matter of years to come about.

The room in which the drying was done had long hot pipes, which would sometimes be really red. The heat in here was terrific. Two girls held the job as drying maids, and I think it was a dangerous job, it was so unhealthy. For in wet weather the girls would be in this wet heat nearly all day, drying dozens of sheets and other articles, while in frosty weather the danger was twofold; for the girls would be in this wet heat for long enough to be red faced and bathed in perspiration, then go out of doors to hang clothes in the frosty air.

In fairness to the Home I must say these girls were usually supplied with a woollen garment which they were supposed to put on when they went outside. They were, on washing days, supplied with strengthening soup for supper and mid-morning, and on one day a week they rested in bed until ten in the morning.

Years later, when visiting the Home, I was glad to see the drying room had been done away with, and more up-to-date equipment had taken its place.

When writing about Isabella and the coppers, I had forgotten to mention that I myself once, when taking up a tray full of clothes from the copper, fell – tray and all – into the large rinse tub below. Fortunately the tub had been filled with clean fresh water, and though I was bruised, shaken and wet through, nothing worse happened, and after a day or two I recovered from my fright.

One stormy November evening, all the glass skylights that went the length of the ironing room crashed in. Filth and glass lay everywhere, on tables where ironing had been in progress, on the floor, in fact all over the place, and yet not one girl was injured. Somehow, and for some unknown reason, every girl working under that skylight had left her post a second before, either to get a fresh iron or for some other reason. After we had recovered from our shock, the class sister said, 'I think every one must attend evensong tonight and give thanks that nobody was injured.' We cleared up the mess and went to evensong. All I can remember about that service was that somewhere in the Psalm came these words: 'Make them afraid with thy storm.'

I did not leave the Home when I was fourteen as would

normally be the case if I had stayed the usual time of two years. The Sister Superior felt I was too young to go to service.

Just before I was fifteen, this lady sent for me and said, 'I have heard of a good post for you, Emma. We are sending you to a vicarage in a Cornish village. One of our girls holds the post as cook there and I am sure she will look after you. You will be house-parlourmaid and will receive nine pounds a year.'

I did not then realize how much I loved the Home, and I was just excited that I was to go back to my native county.

The dismissal service was said over me by the chaplain at evensong the evening before I left. I had a box of clothing, all useful serviceable things; but alas! my outdoor clothing, all black and plain, told all and sundry that I had come from a Home.

CHAPTER 12

Re-Entering the World

IT WAS IMPRESSED UPON ME BEFORE I LEFT THAT I WAS NEVER
to talk about the Home or let anyone know where I had come
from. Now, indeed, my troubles began. Now at last I realized
what it meant to be sent to a penitentiary at the age of twelve.
I had been young enough to become deeply attached to the
Home and to all who had shown me kindness. Even when,
after a few months, one of the other girls had impressed upon
me what the Home was for, and that it was a penitentiary,
explaining what the word meant, I soon recovered from the
shock by remembering how dear the place and certain people
were to me. So that, beyond brooding over the matter for a
few hours, I had thought no more of it. Now here at last it was
rubbed into me that it was something to be very ashamed of
that I had been an inmate of the Home at Bramshot. It was
just as if a girl had been told that her school or college was
to be something which she could never discuss among her
friends, as it was a matter of disgrace and shame that she had
ever been there.

This then was the first of my troubles on entering the
world. As I have said, my clothing at once stamped me as a
Home girl, so that what was more natural than that people
of the village should be curious as to where I had come from,

and as I could never satisfy their curiosity the worst was conjectured.

There was a thrill in the journey the day I left the Home, and as I neared Cornwall I looked for familiar landmarks. I passed through Plymouth and wished I could see Grandfather, but my mother did not enter my head. It was dark when I arrived at my destination, and there was a pony and trap to meet me.

The driver was a man from the village where I was now to live. The clip-clop of the pony's footsteps under the clear starlit sky was romantic, or seemed so to one who had not been out in the dark for three years. Presently the driver asked, 'Whereabouts in Bramshot did you live?' Now here at once was a difficulty. I sensed that he knew the place and could see I came from a Home. I can't remember what I replied, but I was already wishing I was safely back where I had come from.

It was a long drive to the vicarage, during which I was asked many questions by this man who, by now, I was certain could guess all my history. We reached the vicarage at last and I was thankful to sit in the warm kitchen where Kate the cook had tea ready for me.

From the first I was unhappy; nothing was as I imagined it. The vicar was blessed with an unholy temper. His wife did not get on with her husband and took no pains to hide the fact. Kate (who had also come from Bramshot and who, I had been told, had been a very good girl there and would help me) was anything but helpful. Altogether I was homesick, disillusioned and miserable. I longed for the Home. I longed for the sisters. There was nobody I could turn to for help.

The Church was a long way from the vicarage, and when I left Church on Sunday evenings, young people in the congregation looked contemptuously at me and my severe black clothing. I am sure they knew I was a Home girl.

Every day when I went to my room to wash and change

into my afternoon dress, I threw myself on to the bed weeping bitterly. I tried to figure life out. 'Why, oh why,' I kept asking myself, 'had my life been so full of stigmas? – first illegitimacy, then my place of birth being a workhouse, and now for the rest of my life I must always be trying to hide the fact that I had spent years in a penitentiary.' It was so difficult to do this anyway, for I was always being asked where I had come from. When I was actually in the Home there seemed no stigma to it. I had felt surrounded by love and security; and now it was all gone.

My early life of wandering began to have the effect of making me restless, and suddenly I made up my mind that I would run away again. I had been in my place a few months so that, in spite of the fact that I was a perfect fool where money was concerned, never having learnt how to handle it, I had got a few shillings in my purse. I had to fetch the milk each morning from a long distance, and one morning instead of getting the milk, I walked to the railway station and booked a seat to Plymouth. I determined to go to Grandfather.

When I arrived at my grandfather's home, my mother had already been to see him, waving a telegram she had received from my mistress, asking if I had arrived there.

I forgot to state before that my mother had written, or rather got somebody else to write to me while I was at the vicarage, having obtained my address from Grandfather, so that my mistress knew her address.

Grandfather's new wife was kind enough to give me a meal, but she was a very righteous woman and made me feel I had been very wrong indeed to take such a step. I felt now, too, that I had been, and began to wish myself back in the vicarage.

Looking back, I think I might have done quite well at the vicarage had I not been worried with the problem of having to keep silent about the very place and people I most longed to discuss. Also I should have had far more chance of getting on if the other girl had not been there. Whereas I

was one of the girls at Bramshot who was always getting into
hot water for some trivial offence or breach of rule, this girl
had gone through the Home without one black mark against
her. She had won her first-class cap at eight months instead
of the usual twelve, and altogether had been considered a
shining light in the Home, so that the Sister Superior had
really thought it was a splendid chance for me to be placed
under her. But it did not turn out that way and I often found
myself being blamed by her for things she had done.

Altogether, the young woman was not what she seemed
at the Home to be; after I had run away, I felt very bitter as I
read the letter that Sister Superior sent me later.

When reproaching me, she said sadly, 'And I am sure
you had a wonderful help and good example in Kate.' What
reply could I make? For even in my sordid upbringing I had
early learnt the lesson of not telling tales out of school.

Another cause for my unhappiness had been the vague
disillusionment caused by my master and mistress's behaviour
to each other. In the Home it had been an unwritten law that
clergy and ladies, whether sisters or merely lady visitors, were
perfect people. No doubt they did not consider themselves
such, but somehow I got the general impression that no lady
could ever do or say anything wrong, and that all priests were
saints. Now I was quickly undeceived.

Altogether the change was too great for my mental balance.
Now, here I was at my Grandfather's home being scolded,
while dear Grandfather turned his sightless face towards us
and listened helplessly.

'You had better go to the Refuge,' Grandfather's wife
said, 'they will find you another job. There's no room for you
here, and I know your mother can't have you.'

So I made my way to the Refuge, where I was taken in.
The matron of this Refuge was a very severe-looking person,
and her voice matched her face. After lecturing me, she said,
'I will send for your box, and we must try you in another place.

It will be difficult to place you, for of course we cannot ask your late mistress for a character under the circumstances.'

I don't remember very much about the Refuge. I was only there a few days, but it seemed a place where policemen brought girls off the streets, and I know these girls were sent to Homes from there. As far as my memory goes there was much tear-shedding and misery.

A few days after I had entered the Refuge, the matron called me down from upstairs where I was very busy house-cleaning. 'Emma, come down at once, I want you!' called that voice I had learned to dread. 'You are going to a situation at a boarding house on the sea-front as general servant,' she said. She added, 'You will only have eight pounds a year now, for after your behaviour you cannot choose the kind of place you'd like.'

My heart sank in my boots at her tone. It sank still lower, when I was introduced to my new mistress. I shall call her Mrs Turner. She was a woman in her fifties and if ever there was a hard woman, she was one. The house was huge, she had many lodgers, and I, who was only fifteen, had to do all the dirty work of that house; there were no labour-saving appliances. Some of the rooms were large and covered all over with coconut matting. Mrs Turner would stand over me as I broomed these until my hands were covered in blisters.

I shared a small bedroom in the basement next to the kitchen with her niece, whom Mrs Turner assured me was a 'married lady' and must be treated with great respect. Actually she was separated from her husband and was being exploited by her aunt for her own purposes.

'All tips will be shared between you,' said Mrs Turner. (I never saw any.) I was given the scraps from the lodgers' plates for my meals, and my inside revolted. I have never been to prison, that is one experience I have so far been spared; but I am perfectly certain that the lot of a prisoner would be infinitely preferably to my life in that household.

Mrs Turner's husband I remember as a poor hen-pecked

fellow who was terrified of his domineering wife. Once or twice this poor man had, out of compassion, offered me a cup of tea when he made one for himself and his wife in the morning. Nothing could escape her eagle eye, and in each case we were caught, and she would be in a towering rage, saying the most insulting things to us both. The niece would pretend to sympathize with me, then repeat to her aunt anything I might say.

I was so utterly wretched now that I often dwelt on the idea of committing suicide. Looking back then to my days at the vicarage it seemed like heaven, and I wished with all my heart I had not been so foolish as to run away. I was in the same town that contained my Grandfather and all my people, yet I felt utterly friendless and alone. Escape from this terrible woman I must at all costs; but how? I was never allowed outside the place. Mrs Turner watched me like a hawk.

Then one day, in a frenzy, I escaped through the back gate in my working dress, just as I was. For a while I looked about me, wondering where to turn. Every policeman I saw frightened me because I thought they must know I had run away from my place. It was, I knew, no use going to my people. At last I decided to throw myself on the mercy of the matron at the Refuge; though I feared her, it was not with such an overwhelming fear as I had for Mrs Turner.

The matron was terribly angry with me. She made me feel that now she was certain of what she had suspected all along, that I was a thorough bad lot, and that nothing further could be done about me. As if she thought it was the most dreadful punishment that could be inflicted, she said severely, 'We must get your box back, and I shall write to the Sister Superior at Bramshot and see if they will take you back, for I can't keep you here. I'm quite sure the Committee would never allow it, and we certainly could not put you into service again.'

Though the Matron did not realize it, the mention of the possibility that I might return to Bramshot was at least a ray of hope in this dark world in which I now found myself. Nothing could make me regret having run away from Mrs Turner, for the woman treated me shamefully. I had slaved for her from early morning until late at night, all day and every day, for the few weeks I was there. Not one kind word had I had from her; never an outing, or anything that could lighten my existence. Yet as she stood over me, making me slave until the sweat poured off me, she would assure me again and again that it was lucky for me that she was employing me. Not many people, she said, are willing to employ bad girls from Homes, especially if they have already run away from one place.

I could not tell the Matron these things, for she would not listen to anything I had to say. If she had listened, I am quite sure she would not have believed me. I am sure that the only reason Mrs Turner employed a Home girl was because she could get her cheaper, and she must have known that no girl who had people to care for her would for one moment stay under her roof.

For the day or so I spent at the Refuge, the Matron was pointedly cold and severe when addressing me. Prostitutes brought in out of the night were treated with more kindness.

Just a few days of this and, merciful Heaven!, I was informed that the Sister Superior at Bramshot would take me back. When I entered the gate of the convent drive I could have kissed the very ground, so great was my relief at being back again.

I was placed at the bottom of the laundry class as if I had never been there before. Sisters and other former friends received me coldly. There was, for a time, many hurtful references to my being a 'failure'. I couldn't get on outside, etc. etc.

I bore it all without a murmur. There was nothing I could say, for as far as the vicarage was concerned, I felt I had done very wrongly indeed, and that I fully deserved everyone's criticism. And how could I tell them all of the other dreadful place? Even if I had been believed, I should quite rightly be told that had I stayed at the vicarage, I should never have been placed with Mrs Turner.

I lived it down in time. Gradually the love and friendship I had known and valued before came back. I soon found myself higher in class, and I worked with a will.

Soon after my return, I made a full confession and explained to the chaplain all that had worried me hitherto; and now at last I was mentally free, with a quiet inward happiness I had never known before.

CHAPTER 13

I Return to the Convent

THE YEARS PASSED. I GREW IN BODY AND IN SOME WAYS IN mind. I say in some ways, for as I realized years later when I entered the world for good, I was very ignorant of many things, and, of course, of the world and its ways. Religion and work were the two subjects that I was daily taught. I became very wrapped up in my religion, and the chapel became the centre of my being. This side of me was fostered by my friend, Sister Kate, who for years kept telling me that she was sure I had a vocation to the religious life. And so, as I grew, I awaited my call.

I became an expert laundress, and in this way was a very useful member of the establishment. In time I dressed differently from the other girls, and had privileges such as I had not when in class.

Girls began to enter the Home younger than formerly, though none ever came so young as I had done. The youngest I ever knew was fifteen; the older woman became more rare. Many of these girls had had illegitimate children. As I have said elsewhere, it was forbidden to talk of one's past life, but now and then a word would be dropped that told one that this or that girl was a mother. In such cases I always wondered what had happened to the poor babe. One woman I shall always hold in my memory with great respect. One could not help knowing that this woman (she was about thirty) had had at least two children, for she made no secret of the matter. She was, however, deeply devoted to her children and was always surreptitiously making little things for them. On one occasion, I remember, she proudly showed a little bonnet she had made for her little girl to Sister Kate in front of us all.

Sister Kate, instead of admiring Hilda's handiwork, looked stern, as she said: 'We don't talk of those things here, Hilda. Put it away at once, please.'

Hilda coloured to the roots of her hair, as she sadly folded her handiwork and put it away in tissue paper with a little lavender bag inside.

I cannot pretend that I liked this girl, for I didn't. There was something about her that repelled me, but she has always been one of those people I have never forgotten. Some time after the bonnet incident, this young woman went on hunger-strike until she was released, for, she said, she must get out to work for her children. I might not like her, but I did like her principles. While she was on hunger-strike she was put into the cell where I had spent one awful night when thirteen years old. This was called the punishment room. It contained a bed and chair, nothing else, one tiny dormer window, high up, that just admitted a view of the sky. Hilda was there for days, refusing all food. Once Sister Kate asked me to take food to her, and asked me to talk to her and see what I could do with her. I held the plate in one hand and a cup of hot tea in the other and – let me admit it – perhaps I felt a little important with my mission.

As I unlocked the door, I saw Hilda, looking thin and gaunt, sitting in the corner of the room. She took the mug of tea out of my hand, then threw it in my face. Fortunately the tea had had time to cool on the journey up the stairs and along the corridors, so that I was not scalded. Strangely enough, I was not angry either. I admired the girl. I made my exit quickly without saying any of the things I had planned to say to her.

I think it was two or three days later that we heard, with relief, that Hilda had got her way, and that the Sister Superior, recognizing at last that the girl's love for her children was genuine, suddenly gave in and gave the girl her promise that she should be sent home immediately if she took a basin of bread and milk. This she did, and I never saw her again.

Somehow I've never been able to forget her. I hope that both she and her little ones found happiness.

I grew into young womanhood with the fixed idea that babies were something that must never be thought of, let alone discussed. Men I separated vaguely into two separate classes – those that one could speak to, and those that one couldn't. The former contained the chaplain, laundryman and the old gardener. None of these were thought of as men at all. One was used to them; they were just there, just as the building itself was there. The latter contained such men as plumbers, or painters; these were men proper, and because we were never allowed to address them, I had a hazy idea that they were sinful creatures who would in some way contaminate one, if given a chance. This was never said: it was what I unconsciously presumed because of the silence that was held between us.

This assumption was all the easier on my part because of my early experience with Pratt and Dusty. For though I never consciously thought of these men nowadays, they and the unnatural way they had treated me as a child were never forgotten.

When dividing men into two groups, if I thought of my grandfather at all, it would, of course, have been to allot him his place among the chaplain, laundryman and gardener group, this group not only being harmless, but each in his own place beneficial to us.

The laundryman almost fell out of his place in the harmless group to take it up in the second doubtful group, when on the date of King George the Fifth's coronation in June, 1911, we were all assembled in the evening on the lawn having a good time. He played the gramophone to us, the first time, by the way, that I had ever heard one. A record of riddles was being played. A voice called across the lawn – 'Why does the Prince of Wales wear blue braces?' Came the answer, equally loud and clear – 'To keep his trousers up.'

The Sister Superior rose hurriedly from her seat, her veil tightly (oh, so tightly) drawn round her, a shocked frown on her beautiful face. She hurried over to the laundryman; the gramophone stopped dead; we heard it no more.

After this, fireworks and balloons were the order of the evening. I am glad to say that the laundryman's momentary fall from grace did not bar him from entertaining us for the rest of the evening. The novelty of our entertainment that evening was quite unique in my memories of the Home.

From time to time a death would occur in the Home. Everyone that could be spared attended the funeral service. On these occasions I dwelt morbidly on the fact that my own death might occur at any time and that therefore I must dwell more and more on religious matters and prepare for the inevitable end. A most unnatural outlook for a girl in her teens, or so I think now.

Sister Kate, whom I continued to love very devotedly, had a great influence over my life. Always she impressed me with her opinion that I had a religious vocation. She suggested that in time I might go abroad as a missionary, working with the Sisters in India or some other country. I became full of religious zeal, dedicating my life for this purpose. I was, I think, nineteen years old when Sister Kate said she would like me to go to one of their hospitals in the county of Berkshire. I was to go, first of all, as head laundrymaid. Later I was to be taken into the wards, taught nursing, then in due course I should be able to go abroad as a missionary.

The thought of my holy vocation sustained me through the difficult period of parting from Sister Kate and other dear friends, and from the Home itself. Before I left, Sister Kate said, 'Oh, Emma, don't let Sister Grace, who is in charge of the hospital laundry, worry about your pale face. You must explain to her that you are really quite well and strong.'

'All right, Sister,' I said. Then she kissed me affectionately, and I took my place in the cab that was to take me to the station.

Alas for my second attempt to enter the world. I went one way, my box went the other. I was in the right train all right; it was the box that had got labelled wrongly. When I arrived at the hospital everything had to be lent to me right down to a nightgown.

This was in January. The whole hospital, it seemed, was suffering from influenza. I fell ill at once. I had no temperature, so that nobody recognized the fact that I was ill. I could eat nothing or hardly anything. I had an awful pain somewhere in the chest, indigestion it was called. I was given bicarbonate of soda, etc., but no, that awful pain would not move. To make matters worse, the laundry, which was much smaller than the one to which I was accustomed, not only had the windows shut all the time, but cracks and anything that might have let in a little life-giving air were stuffed with rags or paper so that I felt the whole time that I wanted to gasp for air. When, as head laundress, I suggested we might let a little air in, the laundry girls under me were shocked and reminded me that the windows were *never* interfered with. I felt too ill to argue.

We had a small dining-room near the hospital kitchen. I think there were about twenty maids all told; or perhaps not quite as many as that. Anyhow, one of the elder maids one morning remarked in a shocked voice, 'Doesn't that new laundress look ill?'

One of the younger laundry girls at once said, 'Oh, I heard her tell Sister Grace that she is always pale like that, and that she is really quite well and strong.'

I held my peace. I felt so ill that I wished I could die. But it was true I had said that on my first evening, and anyhow these servants were all strangers to me. It was, I felt, no use trying to tell anyone how I felt. I forgot all about my vocation. I could not work; I got weaker and weaker. At last I just begged that I might be sent back to Bramshot. I am not sure, but I think they thought I was thoroughly lazy.

Anyhow I was returned to Bramshot. I had only been away a short time, and on the way back I missed my connexion in London, which meant that I had to go by a much later train, so that I arrived at the Home that night very late. Sister Kate had been waiting up for me, and as I stumbled through the heavy front door, ill and tired, she spoke gently, 'My dear child, how late you are! '

I think she was almost as glad to have me back as I was to get back. I did not, however, return to normal health simply because I had returned to Bramshot. I was weak and ill for many weeks, but whenever the Sister Superior took my temperature she was puzzled, for I never had a high temperature once. I could not digest my food at all, and I was always vomiting some dark substance, but I did not tell the sisters this. I felt it was my duty to say that I was better whenever I was asked, so I suppose that is why I did not get proper attention, for I did not see a doctor the whole time I was ill. Moreover, I worked or tried to work all the time. As I have said, everyone except Sister Kate thought I had suddenly become very lazy.

Sister Kate sent me to lie down each day after dinner for a while. I dreaded this, however, for on rising again I always felt so much weaker.

It was after Easter when Sister Superior decided that if I did not get stronger soon I must see a doctor. By this time I was improving so that I did get better without medical aid. I think now that I had had gastric ulcers. For some years after this I would get a little return of the trouble from time to time, but each attack was less severe.

145

*   *   *

I settled down again for a few more years. When I had fully recovered from my illness I once again became a valuable and cheerful worker.

In the Convent we knew very little of what was taking place in the outside world, for we never saw a newspaper. It was the fourth of August, 1914 when, in the early morning before the girls came down to work in the laundry, I stepped outside to get some coke for the laundry fire and the old gardener shuffled up to me and said in a dramatic tone, 'England declared war with Germany last night, twelve o'clock!'

His tone sent a shudder down my spine. The news was so unexpected here in this corner of the globe, where we never read the daily papers.

The sisters, I suppose, had a paper, for the news did not seem such a bombshell as it would have been had they been as ignorant of the country's affairs as I was. Very soon we had gathered in the chapel for a service of intercession.

My mother sometimes wrote to me these days; she seemed anxious to be friends. I could, however, feel no affection for her, yet I did sometimes reply to her letters, reminding myself that after all she was my mother. Through mother's letters, or rather the letters that somebody would write on her behalf, I knew that my brother, Harry, and my half-brother, Willie, were both serving their country. Harry was in the Navy, and Willie in the Army. Naturally I was proud of the fact. We were told a little news from time to time.

I seem to remember that the sisters talked a great deal about 'the Angels of Mons', as though some great modern miracle had taken place; and hosts of angels were seen to be fighting on our side. I am afraid that I was sceptical about the whole thing, so perhaps that is why I can't remember the story very clearly.

Names of warriors who were related to us were read aloud at Mass each day for intercession, my brothers among them. This gave us a feeling that somehow, in some small way, we were taking part in the war. If prayers were of any avail, then we were doing our part.

We certainly did more than our part where self-denial was concerned; for our rations were cut down to the bare necessities, and I, for one, often found it difficult to keep up my strength for the hard and strenuous work I had to perform in the laundry. For a while, I was matron of the wash-house and worked harder than any of my girls.

The following Good Friday I was sitting in chapel, taking part in the three hours' service, when through the open chapel door I heard the front door bell ring. Some strange presentiment told me that that bell had some connexion with me. A few minutes later a hand was placed on my shoulder and, looking up, I saw the Sister Superior. 'Come outside,' she whispered.

I followed her wonderingly. I turned the corner of the passage, and saw, sitting on the same window ledge where so many years before I had seen Grandfather and Harry, a tall good-looking sailor.

I hesitated; then Sister Superior turned to me with a smile: 'Don't you remember your brother, Harry?' she said.

I went over to him shyly, yet proudly. He was a young man of nineteen then and very good-looking, as I have already said. We went over to the Cottage for tea and a chat, then dear Harry took his leave. I watched him ride down the drive on his bicycle. He looked over his shoulder and waved farewell. I never saw him again.

I could not get my handsome brother out of my head. I thrilled with pride every time I thought of him. I pondered, too, on the war, and all that it meant to such men as Harry. His ship had taken part in the battle of the Falkland Islands. All he could or would say about it was, 'It was a terrible sight to see men struggling in the water.' We had such a short time together, so that we did not discuss for long a subject that had such horrible memories for him.

In the summer of 1917, when Sister Kate was away on

her rest, I received a letter from my mother, in which she informed me that Harry's ship had been torpedoed in home waters. Everyone on the boat was killed, and close relations had had to go and identify their loved ones. Mother had just had a new baby, so that my stepfather, who was in the Army but home on leave, went to the port where the tragedy had taken place. He was accompanied by his own eldest son, my half-brother, Willie, who had also got a few days' leave. There they identified all that remained of my handsome sailor brother.

I could hardly read the rest of the letter, I was so upset. True, Harry and I had grown up separately, but just then all that he had meant to me in those early years at Redruth Church town came back with vivid tender memories. I saw again the little fair-haired boy who had just been breeched, standing on the chair, surrounded by admiring Union children. I saw him plunging his head in that well at the bottom of the hill when we had both been scolded by the angry neighbours, who kept calling us bastards. I pictured us both at Grandfather's knee, and then playing together outside that dear cottage. I even pictured the scene at the round table in the living-room, when we always quarrelled about our basins of bread and milk or kettle broth, each accusing the other of having the most. Now he was gone, bastard or no bastard. He had given his life that others might live.

It was a long time before I could finish the letter, but at last I read these words: 'I shall miss Harry's allowance now, so will you come out into the world and earn some money and help your mother?'

The friend of my girlhood, 'Sister Kate', was away. I could not discuss the matter with her as I should otherwise have done. Had I been able to do so, the rest of my story would, I am quite sure, have a different ending, better or worse I cannot say.

*   *   *

A new novice had lately come to work at Bramshot. She was in charge of the laundry. When she overheard me talking to one of the lay sisters of my trouble, addressing me, she said: 'Emma, if you do decide to go into the world, I would so like you to go to my mother. She needs a house-parlourmaid, and I know I could recommend you.'

I had never had to make any decision for myself, and Sister Kate was not there to decide for me, so I just let things happen automatically. 'I'll go to your mother,' I said.

Before I left the Convent, Sister Kate returned. She was hurt and even a little angry that all this had been arranged (as she put it) 'behind her back'. 'It is not at all the sort of thing I should have chosen for you,' she said.

Once again I bade goodbye to my old friends.

CHAPTER 14

Out in the World

I WAS MET IN LONDON BY MY MASTER AND ONE OF HIS daughters. I felt hopelessly bewildered on the busy station and do not think I should ever have managed had I not been met. Mr Thomas very kindly pointed out certain places of interest, but I was so confused with everything that I took very little in.

We arrived later at the suburban house that was to be my future home. My new mistress received me in a kind but dignified manner. All I could think of saying was, 'What a tiny little house!' which was not at all the sort of remark I ought to have made.

'Come along to the kitchen,' Mrs Thomas said, 'and I will introduce you to Winnie.' Winnie was the cook-general.

This girl reminded me of the girls at Bramshot when they first came. She had an unkempt look about her. 'Good evening,' she said, graciously.

When we were alone, I had a shock. Winnie said, 'Mrs Thomas has asked me to be very kind to you because you have come from a Home.'

Considering I had been working as a matron in the laundry of that Home for years past, it was a bit of a come-down to be spoken to by this girl in this condescending manner. However, I tried not to mind and set myself the task of making myself at home, for I was determined that this time I would make a success of living out in the world. It was hard for a time, apart from my fellow-servant's condescending manner. The daughters of the house treated me in the oddest way until they became accustomed to me. If I met one of them on the stairs, she would look at me suspiciously, as if she thought I might have the silver concealed about my person. I am quite sure they thought it their duty to watch me closely in case I stole or committed some other grave offence. After a short while, however, their attitude underwent a change and they realized at last that even though I might have come from a penitentiary, I was yet quite a normal person.

Winnie invited me to her home one day. It was such a slum that it reminded me of Mrs Pratt's tenement-room at Plymouth, and I did not go again. This girl left shortly after this and I was the only maid kept. I now enjoyed privileges that had not been possible before, and I settled down happily enough.

It was a whole month before I was in the position to help my mother at all. I sent her what I could spare, but I had no idea at all of the value of money, and as my wages were not high, I very soon found myself penniless again, and had to wait until another pay day before I could even purchase stamps. I had only been with Mr and Mrs Thomas a short while and helped my mother very little, when Mr Thomas told me bluntly that I was foolish to send money to her. 'She is nothing to you,' he said.

I could not in those days think for myself, and what Mr Thomas said seemed to me to be a command. So I did not send again – and when one remembers that it was for this very purpose that I had left the Convent and friends that I loved!

Though I had settled down, I still hankered after the life to which I was accustomed, and as Sister Kate's letters to me still hinted, from time to time, that she was sure I had a vocation to the religious life, I decided to try another convent in a different community of Sisters. Sister Kate made the necessary arrangements, and it was decided I should enter the Convent of All Hallows at Ditchingham in Norfolk, on my twenty-fifth birthday.

Mrs Thomas said to me a few days before I left, 'Look, Emma, we have had your uniform all laundered and shall keep it until you come back to us.'

I was hurt and replied, 'I shall never come back. You know I'm going to be a sister.'

She smiled, knowingly, as she replaced the dresses and aprons (which I had told her she could give to the next maid) in the drawer from which she had taken them.

One bitterly cold day in January, 1919, I entered the convent at Ditchingham as a postulant. The sisters were aware it was my birthday and my little cell contained many sacred cards with birthday greetings on them. A very kindly gesture, I thought.

This convent was very different from the one in which I had grown up. To begin with, it was not a penitentiary, though there was a penitentiary near. This was the community house and only sisters lived here.

The rule of life was much stricter than I had been accustomed to, and the services in chapel seemed to be much higher and more closely related to a Roman Catholic form of worship.

Everybody from the Reverend Mother downwards was extremely kind to me, especially the Novice Mistress, for I was the only postulant at that time in her care, and she went out of her way to encourage and help me. Nevertheless, I soon began to doubt my vocation. I came to the conclusion that it was just my love for the sisters at Bramshot and the undue influence of Sister Kate that I had confused with a call from God. I am thankful to say that both the chaplain and the Reverend Mother came to the same conclusion, for one day after I had served three months as a postulant, the Reverend Mother sent for me. This lady told me in the kindest way possible that she and the chaplain had had a talk about me, and had decided that my place was in the world. 'Your vocation, my child,' she said, 'is to be a wife and mother. And,' she added sweetly, 'a very good wife and mother you will make.'

A thrill went through me at her words. Here was something that had never before been suggested. A wife and mother! Was it possible? Suddenly, in my mind's eye, I saw a little home, furniture, curtains, a cradle – and I tried to imagine (only this was more difficult) a man in slippers.

Before I left Mr and Mrs Thomas, she had said, 'If you find you have made a mistake, come back to us.' So now I wrote to her and received a letter by return of post: 'Dear Emma, we shall be very glad to have you back again.' I picked up my life where I had left off on my birthday. As Mrs Thomas had expected, I did need that uniform again.

Shortly after my return, Mrs Thomas told me that the gardener that used to work for them before the war was now coming back. 'I expect you'll fall in love with him,' she said.

With these and the Reverend Mother's recent words still ringing in my ears, what more natural than that a few months after the return of this gardener, we were engaged to be married. It was April, 1920, when we became engaged, and after a year of quiet courtship, during which time I visited his people in a delightful thatched cottage in Essex, we were married from my employers' house. So then I became a wife.

My husband and I were an odd pair. He was and is (for, thank God, he is still living) a simple countryman; while I was, and still am, such a complex piece of machinery that I cannot understand myself, let alone expect others to do so.

Our early married life was not ideally happy. I had been used to such large numbers for so many years. Now I was missing much of which I felt a need, though I cannot put a name to it. My husband is an excellent gardener, but when not at work, he usually sleeps; so that married life seemed to me a very lonely existence.

If I have spoken very little of our courtship, it is because I hardly know myself how it all came about. I remember a remark one of my young ladies made to me one day: she said – 'If you have two servants, a man and a woman, the thing to do is to marry them up. Then you have two servants for the price of one.'

I often recalled that remark in later years. I think it was suggested so often that I should fall in love with this gardener (a man fourteen years older than myself) that in the end I think I believed myself in love; and I am sure I must have taken the initiative, for I am quite certain my shy husband would never have had the pluck to make a direct proposal. Anyhow, we drifted into this engagement and once engaged, I could never find the courage to break it off and admit the whole thing was a mistake. Though I am bound to admit, there were many times when I felt it was.

After our wedding we went to Hastings for a week's honeymoon. On the table in the bed-sitting-room we had booked for the week a letter lay. It was addressed to me in Sister Kate's handwriting. She said that I was in her thoughts and prayers, and that she was quite sure that God's blessing had been upon our marriage that day. That letter was the nicest memory of my honeymoon week.

Yes, I know that sentence looks very odd in cold print, but this is a true story, and I must speak the truth. Yet before I go further, I am bound to say that however unromantic my husband may have been, I was really very lucky in the man I married. Quiet, industrious, sober and faithful, he has worn far better than perhaps a man of my own temperament would have done. A family doctor of ours, who was a friend of several years' standing, once said to me, 'It is a good thing that you married a man so entirely different to yourself, for if you were both alike, the roof would come off.' I'm not quite sure what he meant by this remark, but I've a pretty good idea and I think he was right.

September, 1922, saw the birth of my first child, a girl. I had prepared lovingly and carefully for the great event. Most of her little garments I made myself by hand, and I was very proud when somebody who had been carefully examining the layette exclaimed, 'You could not have prepared more carefully had you been expecting a little princess.'

Well, when she arrived that Saturday morning in the private nursing home in which I had booked a bed months before, she was indeed a princess to me. I had never had anything to do with babies, and now I thought I had never seen anything so perfect. 'Why!' I exclaimed to nurse in surprise and delight, 'Isn't she wonderful? She has even got nails.'

'H'm! She'd be much more wonderful if she hadn't,' said nurse.

What a picture was the Moses cradle I had trimmed all in blue! (I had hoped for a boy.) We had not yet got a home of our own, for after our wedding I had continued to work and we lived in the house. I now became restless and ambitious on my baby's account. I wanted something better for her than what my own life had been.

Just at that time there were many posters around inviting young willing workers to come to Australia. I turned this over in my mind. I remembered hearing that my mother's brother, who had emigrated to Australia when I was a baby, had done very well out there. He had married, had a large family of boys, and been able to give them all a good education, besides buying his own house. Why, I thought, should we not do the same?

I talked it over with my husband. What I needed was a man who was master in his own house; one who could not only arrange his own life, but upon whom I could lean. Instead of this, I always had to take the leading role. My early life of unsettled wanderings was taking effect, now that I was away from the anchorage of love and security that the life in the Convent gave.

'All right,' said this man of mine. 'We will go, if you like.'

So I set the necessary machinery into motion, and in due course we were told on what ship and what date we were to sail.

We were to sail on the S.S. *Euripides* of the Aberdeen line at the end of August, 1923. Baby was nearly a year old when we left our native shores.

Before we sailed I felt I should like to have the opportunity of getting to know my mother a little. I should, I felt, in all probability never see her again. So I wrote to her and asked if she could put us up for two or three weeks before we sailed, for I knew that by now her circumstances had greatly improved, and that she probably had room for us. I made financial arrangements so that we should not be a burden to her. I was anxious also to show off my wonderful new possession, this blue-eyed baby of mine.

Mother replied that she and my stepfather would be pleased to have us. Then I packed up a tea-chest of useful articles, such as household linen, which I sent her in advance. This, I felt, would not only be a help to her, but would ensure greater comfort for ourselves while under her roof. Mother, by this time, had brought up a large family; each one as they came on had had a better time of it than the last. She knew – oh, yes, she knew how to handle babies. Before I knew where I was, I was experiencing the most awful pangs of jealousy at the way Mother was handling this her first grandchild, and at the way that grandchild – my own precious babe – was snuggling up to her granny.

My stepfather was a changed man. The war had robbed him of his strength, but had given him a pension which meant a little security. He was kinder now, and he, too, took to my

156

little one. He talked to her and played with her in a way her good father could never do.

Mother's living-room then was homely and nice to see. Family photographs were all over the place. There was dear Harry in his sailor's uniform, looking down upon us from the wall. There was Willie in Army uniform doing the same. There was my little sister (or I should say half-sister) and two or three more younger brothers. The mahogany chest of drawers I mentioned earlier was not there yet, for Grandfather was still living then. Homely touches were everywhere.

Our bedroom was homely, too. The youngest member of the family, whom I will call Frank, was then a boy of nine, a good scholar at school, neat and well-dressed, and good mannered. I loved him at once. (I will anticipate my story here to say that this boy has for several years now been a high-ranking officer in the Royal Artillery.)

Mother and I did not hit it off very well. I think even her affectionate ways with my baby irritated me, irrational though that may seem. The thought of all I had missed myself, and with what indifference she had treated me, her own child, would keep thrusting its ugly memory between us. Yet I was pleased also that my little one should be loved by Mother and her husband, for it all made a touch of homeliness, the memory of which is a pleasant one to look back upon.

There was one remark that Mother used sometimes to make, as if talking to herself. This would be – 'I've been a good mother to *all* my children.' Needless to say I found it very difficult not to tell her just what sort of a mother she had been to me, her eldest. Mostly I held my tongue, for the slightest reference to my childhood was enough to send Mother into a towering rage.

This is still true today, and it is true, too, that when I go to see her (as I do on rare occasions), she will make that same remark. I know now that poor Mother feels guilty when I am around and she makes this remark because she is trying to convince herself that she has been a good mother to me as well as to the others. I wonder if she says it many more times, she will succeed in convincing herself? If so, I will not begrudge her the peace of mind it will bring, for she is now an old woman; the past is past and cannot be recalled.

While we were at Plymouth we called to see my grandfather who was now bedridden. My husband and I had for months past been sending Grandfather two and sixpence a week through a Salvation Army officer. Not that we could really afford it, but I was very anxious to make the old man's last days as comfortable as possible, and when my husband knew all that Grandfather had meant to me in my earliest years, he consented that I should send this money. I now realize how good of him it was. Grandfather's second wife was dead now. There was the poor blind man, who had outlived two wives, and was now dependent upon one of his daughters to come in and do what was necessary for him. The old man had fallen into the habit that old people sometimes get, and kept repeating himself, 'How old is the baby?' he asked again and again, as he clutched her little fingers, for she was sitting on the bed.

'Ten months, Grandad,' I replied, as often as the question was asked, and each time would be forthcoming, 'Well – her grandmother walked when she was ten months old.'

His great-grand-daughter, who had no intentions whatever of following such a wonderful example, at last clamoured to be taken up, so we took our leave of the old man; but not before he said – 'You've both been good to me; I shall miss that bit of money each week.' I kissed my grandfather for the last time, for I did not see him again.

CHAPTER 15

Off to Australia

AT LAST THE DAY CAME WHEN WE WERE TO SAIL FROM OUR native shores for the far-off promised land of Australia. A Salvation Army officer, who was stationed at Cape Town and had been over here for a few months' holiday with his wife and daughter, was embarking on the same boat. A group of Salvationists were singing the mournful notes of 'God be with you till we meet again'. Somehow it brought a lump to one's throat.

Not that I could feel very sentimental about leaving my stepfather, but I had in this short while grown fond of that little brother, and after all – this *was* my native land. It contained such places as Redruth Church town, and the Convent at Bramshot, that I now looked upon as 'the old home'.

At last we were safely on board. The stewardess was kindness itself. She brought me some hot water to make baby's feed, so I fed her and made her comfortable, and soon the roll of the ship told us we were moving out to sea.

We were somewhere at sea between Teneriffe and Cape Town when suddenly one day I was aware of a sudden rush to one side of the liner. 'Man overboard,' went up a cry. One male passenger jumped over the side; then another; then a third. A member of the crew, who had been cleaning one of the boats, had fallen into the sea. We were in shark-infested waters, but without hesitation these three passengers had dived in that dangerous sea to save the poor seaman. It took time for the liner to come to a standstill and for boats to be lowered. Meantime I, with others, rushed up on to the top deck in order to scan the water for the unfortunate man. Of all those hundreds of passengers, I myself was the first to see that white floating face, and in a flash I was certain it was all over with him. 'There he is! There he is!' I screamed excitedly, pointing to the body. 'Where? Where?' came the cry of the boats' crews who were searching. Then one of them spotted him, and before any time at all they had hauled the poor fellow into the boat.

For three hours after the man was brought up on to the liner deck, the doctor and dispenser tried artificial respiration; but their efforts were all in vain. As far as was known he had no family or friends to mourn for him.

The following day the poor fellow was buried at sea. The sad business cast a gloom over the whole ship.

In due course we arrived at Cape Town. It was dusk as we anchored and I always remember a trivial thing that was so comforting – various signs in flashing coloured electric light bulbs could be seen in the distance. When, presently, I traced the homely familiar word B-O-V-R-I-L, it looked so English, and gave me a feeling that we were not after all so very far away from our native land.

That night we had a concert on board when a gold watch that had been made ready for the occasion at a Cape Town jeweller's was presented to the passenger that first jumped overboard at the time of the tragedy.

Six weeks, or thereabouts, after we had set sail from England, we landed at Albany in Western Australia. My husband had paid for our passage and we had intended to look for work on our arrival. Great was our surprise when our names were read out with those of other emigrants who were directed where to go and what to do. Without exception, these others had had their fares paid by the government, though we learned later that it had to be paid back in a certain number of years.

I think we were relieved, as much as surprised, when we knew that the Australian Government had removed the burden of responsibility from our shoulders, in that our immediate future was to be organized and arranged for us.

The first thing we had to do was to buy travelling rugs, for we had a night's train journey before us. Sleeping berths were provided, but the rugs were our only covering. We travelled all night on what was rightly described as a 'bone-shaker'; sleep was impossible. If one did drop off for a minute or so, the train would stop with a great deal of noise and somebody's name would be called out. Some young man would step out and join the farmer, or whoever it was, that had undertaken to give him employment. Doors would bang, and once more we were on the way.

At Perth we had an early cup of tea on the station, then embarked on another train for a further short journey back to Fremantle. At Albany, the immigration officer had come aboard and given us all instructions as to our immediate future. My husband and I were to go up on the Peel estate, near Fremantle. This was a part of the Australian Government's group settlement scheme. There were several groups on the estate, each group consisting of twenty families. For two weeks, mothers and children were to stay at the immigration homes (unless they made private arrangements) while the menfolk would go right away on to the group, where they would live under canvas for those two weeks and make a clearing in the Bush and erect a hut for each family. When this was accomplished, the women and children were to be fetched to join husbands and fathers. Each family would occupy one of these huts until such time as a bungalow could be built for it. The twenty men would work under the expert direction of an Australian foreman, clearing the virgin soil.

The Government allowed each family three pounds a week to cover the cost of living. This arrangement was to go on for the space of three years, after which time each family should be settled on its own farm and be making it pay. After this each man was to pay back the Government, thirty years being allowed for this.

Thus our future was made clear to us. We knew now that we should benefit from having paid our fare, for our debt to the Australian Government would not be so great as would be the case if we had travelled free.

I decided that, for the time being, I had had enough of my fellow passengers. These women had each other to talk things over with, and they went out in parties of twos and threes, while I would stand on the beach alone staring out to sea with a lump in my throat, as I remembered that twelve thousand miles now separated me from the two beloved spots that would always hold a special place in my heart – namely, Redruth Church town and the Convent at Bramshot, and oh! that I could see Sister Kate just for one moment, I used to think, longingly.

In due course I joined the other women and children for our journey up to the Bush, thirty miles away, where our menfolk had prepared twenty huts for our reception. Our camp consisted of two rows of huts, ten in each row. Each hut was made of corrugated tin about twelve feet square. Each hut had a doorway but no door, a space for a little window but no window. Each family had bought a bed and other bare necessities in Fremantle. These were now delivered. The men knocked up home-made tables, and we used boxes for chairs; for this way of life was to be only temporary. My husband drove four stakes into the sandy ground which was the only flooring of the hut, and upon this he fixed sacking. This made our child's bed. Some families had as many as three or even four children. The men in these cases fixed up hammocks of sacks, one over the other for them.

My husband and I had brought out a chest of household linen with us. The chest itself made a useful piece of furniture. Covered with a cloth and photographs placed on top, it helped to make the hut look a bit homely.

There was a good cooking stove in each hut; this burnt wood only, and of this we could get as much as we needed. The families, without exception, found the huts unbearably hot with the stove inside, so that the men helped each other to remove them outside the huts. Around the stove each man built a verandah of brushwood. This made an extra room and ensured a certain amount of privacy. We fixed a curtain in the doorway of the hut, and where there were small children, boards also were placed across. This kept the little ones in and the snakes out.

We were thirty miles from Fremantle, and there was no doctor or nurse anywhere near us, and I for one worried much more about baby's welfare than I should have done had I the comforting feeling that help was near in case of necessity. Wireless had been invented before this, but it was not universally used as it is now, and certainly nobody on the estate possessed one, as would be the case in these days when, as I understand, a call by wireless will bring doctor or nurse to the loneliest Bush home.

We had taken our portable gramophone out with us, and very glad of this we were, for we were the only family who had done so. It made the only music there was in the camp, and we were able to give much pleasure to our neighbours in this way.

The Australian Government had arranged for our groceries to be sent up to a nearby camp each week from Charlie Carter's of Fremantle. They were packed in wooden boxes and left at this camp, which had the odd name of 'Thirteen Mile'. I never discovered why it was so called. Our men took it in turns each Friday to drive a horse and cart thither to fetch the goods, at the same time calling at the post office shack for the mail.

No family could run into debt, for the grocery bill was paid each week by the Government and stopped out of the three pound allowance. Each housewife ordered what she needed, but I seem to remember that it was always a shock when we saw how much had been deducted from the pay-packet.

Every Monday, a trap called at the camp with fruit; the driver had a wooden leg, so we naturally called him Peggy. Peggy would sell us a large basket of different kinds of fruit, including grapes, for sixpence. Fresh meat was not obtainable, so we had to live on tinned meat. Occasionally the men would shoot parakeets which swarm in the trees in large numbers. These made a welcome change in the diet. These small parrots made a great din in the trees. I used to wonder what it would sound like if all these birds had been taught to speak as their less fortunate relatives were in captivity.

The time came eventually when the foreman invited the men to draw lots for their land. Some families had many acres allotted to them, but it might be in more than one piece. Also some of the ground might be poor and valueless. Thus to my husband fell one hundred and ten acres in two different lots. After this the men who were keen to get on would spend their spare time on their own ground, clearing the virgin soil and making it ready for vegetation. This reduced the man's debt to the Government, for the more soil he was able to clear himself, the less would have to be done by the body of men who would have to be paid for doing it.

On Sundays men would take their wives and children over to their own land, and while the breadwinner worked away at clearing the soil, the wife would busy herself at sewing or knitting, or spreading a picnic dinner, while keeping an eye on her children.

My husband was older than any of the men, but he was also considered by everyone to be the most hardworking. Not only did he spend much of his spare time on his own land, but I had the largest stock of stacked firewood in the camp. It was amusing to see small lizards slithering in and out of the wood pile, flashing in the strong sunlight.

Some of the women had very little idea of good housekeeping. These women had, for the most part, come from poor districts of London and had had the bad habits of purchasing groceries, etc., in very small quantities, so that they lived from hand to mouth. How to think and order goods for the following week became to them a very difficult task indeed. Thanks to my training in service, this presented no difficulty to me. Those among us who could lay any sort of claim to be good housekeepers were pestered by the others for small loans in the way of tea, sugar, onions, etc., so that when ordering we had to think of others as well as ourselves.

However, not all the good housewives were tolerant all the time, and sometimes there were high words which, in the end, led to better habits.

For a while, bread was delivered once a week from Fremantle. Deliveries ceased, however, as more and more of the wives started to bake their own. Food was indeed a problem, for not only did the ants get everywhere and into everything, but the intense heat soon sent tinned meats and bacon wrong, so that much was wasted in this way and had to be buried. Some of us tried keeping food tied up in butter muslin and suspended in trees. This at least kept flies away from it.

On the night of Christmas Eve, after the sun had gone down and the kiddies were all in bed, we lit a bonfire, and a party of us all sat round it in a ring, singing carols and trying our best to imagine it was midwinter. The moon and stars were always a great comfort to me, for it seemed so wonderful to think that this was the very same moon and those the very same stars that I had loved to watch so long ago as a child away there back in England and twelve thousand miles away. As we sang the old carols that we had learned in childhood, each of us was filled with our own memories, and though our bodies were there under the starlit Australian sky, our minds were thousands of miles away.

On Christmas morning our foreman delivered a Christmas card to each family from the Governor of Western Australia. Our names were written by hand, then printed in gold lettering were the words, 'The Governor and Lady Newdigate offer you and yours their best wishes for a happy Christmas and prosperous New Year'. This card is the only souvenir we have left of our travels, and I treasure it.

So passed Christmas, 1923, the only one we spent down under.

The first Sunday my husband and I went over to our own ground for a day's work and picnic, we had a terrifying experience. My good man was so wrapt up in his work that we had not noticed how late it was getting. When we realized the time, we hurriedly packed up to leave and started out for home. In a few minutes, however, we knew that we were what is known in Australia as being 'bushed'. We walked a few steps this way, then that, taking it in turns to carry the child who seemed to get heavier every minute. We knew the sun would drop very quickly at any minute, and I certainly was terrified as to what would happen to us if we could not at once find our way out of that horrible Bush. Ant hills were everywhere. We could not possibly sit down, let alone lay the child down. There we were, afraid to go on, and still more afraid to stay where we were.

We made up our minds we should have to wander about in circles the whole night through, while the child slept in our arms. Then the sun dropped in the sky and I realized, with relief, what direction we should take, for the sun always set behind our huts. 'Come on!' I said to my husband. He followed thankfully, trusting to my homing instinct. Very soon we saw the lights from the camp; and so – like the old woman in the nursery rhyme – we got home that night.

Now I have to record a really terrifying ordeal, which affected the whole camp.

One Sunday we saw flames and smoke rising from somebody's ground and guessed the horrible truth, that the man or his wife had been careless with a match and had started that terror of all Australians, namely a Bush fire. We hurriedly left our own ground and got back to the camp, where we found a crowd of women and children watching the spread of the flames in fascinated horror. We could hear the loud crackling as more and more brushwood and undergrowth became involved in the flames. To make matters worse, our foreman was away for the weekend, and our men, brave and quick though they were to rush to the scene of the fire, did not really know how to tackle this frightful thing that had sprung upon us so suddenly. The fire had been seen miles away, however, and great was everybody's relief when the foreman from the next group came dashing into the camp on horseback.

He shouted orders to the few men he could see, and very soon every man was dashing out flames with his jacket. In spite of all their efforts, the fire spread fast and furious. Now men dashed back into the camp with orders that we were all to set to at once and pull down our brushwood verandahs, for if the flames spread close to the camp they would most certainly catch fire, and our bits of homes would be destroyed. It looked now as if the fire was going to encircle us completely. I remember putting a few articles of baby clothing in a case together with our bank book and forty pounds in golden sovereigns which we had been hoarding; for by this time I felt pretty certain we should have to fly for our lives.

At the bottom of the camp, not far from the well, we had three or four horses in a roughly made pen. Now we saw the pen had started to burn and horses were prancing and neighing. They were rescued in time, however, and tethered to a safer spot.

It did not, after all, become necessary for us to leave our

huts, for eventually the fire did get under control, but what a miserable picture of blackened ruin it all was. I cannot clearly remember just how many hours the fire had raged, but I can remember sitting with many others after dark watching gum trees that had been burning steadily, now crash down one after the other. It certainly was an interesting sight now that all danger was past.

It is an ill wind that blows nobody any good, and certainly this fire, awful though it had been, considerably lessened the men's debt to the Government, for it cleared the soil in a few hours that would normally have taken the thirty men a few weeks at least. The camp looked bare and miserable now without the primitive verandahs which had made a little homely privacy possible while enjoying fresh air at the same time, while the charred blackened stumps of gum trees, etc., looked very depressing.

In spite of hardships and much physical discomfort, I really liked the life up there in the bush. There was a freedom about it that appealed to me.

I have already stated that we brought our gramophone out with us. This was a continual source of pleasure, not only to ourselves but to the other immigrants.

Among the collection of records I had brought out was one of the song, 'The Bells of St Mary's'. I began to notice that each time I played this record, Jack Miles, who lived a few huts away, invariably came and stood in the doorway listening intently.

Jack had a wife and two children, and while we were fellow passengers on the *Euripides*, I had hardly noticed him or his wife. I had of late, however, become friendly with Mrs Miles, and now in the evening after the day's work was over, I found myself looking forward to Jack appearing in that doorway. In fact I got into the way of putting the record on for the purpose of drawing him. After a little while I found that we got into the habit of looking at each other in the sort of way that sent a thrill through me, such as I had never experienced before. It now dawned upon me that I had fallen head over heels in love with a neighbour's husband.

Jack had a good wife, and he thought the world of his children. I had a good husband and a sweet baby daughter. This thing had to be fought against.

While I was going through a mental conflict over this matter, my husband, who had been suffering a good deal with a skin trouble of his, suddenly announced his intention of returning to England. 'I'm a-going home,' he said, in his countrified way.

Well, this was indeed a bombshell. I was so utterly taken by surprise, for I had never known him to take the initiative before, or if it comes to that, he has never taken it since. I had mixed feelings about the whole thing. I was secretly glad that this husband of mine could make up his mind about something without consulting me. On the other hand, I was enjoying this life out there in the wilds. Yet again, there was a certain amount of relief in the thought that I should no longer have to battle with my feelings for the husband of another woman. Yet it gave me an awful pang of sorrow as I realized that after a few days more, I should never again see Jack framed in that doorway. The attraction was mutual, and there would most certainly be danger to both families had we stayed at the camp. So I took the line of least resistance and let my husband have his way, without trying to influence him in the other direction.

When we told the foreman of his decision, the good man was very sorry indeed for, as he said, he was losing the best worker on the group. At the same time he agreed that his health should come first. 'It was a pity you didn't come out twenty years ago,' he said, 'for it is best to come out young.' Some of the other men and their wives felt a bit homesick when they heard we were returning to England. More than one said that if they had the money they would go also. Perhaps it was just as well they hadn't, for most of them, I've no doubt, made good settlers after the first difficult year or two were passed. There are times when I almost wish that we, too, were penniless at that time, for if we had burnt our boats my husband might have recovered from the skin trouble in time, and perhaps today we might have been well-to-do settlers running our own farm.

Before we left the camp, we gave Jack and his wife our gramophone, and Jack gave me the ditty box which he had used while in the Navy. This I treasure to this day and use it for a workbox.

I stated earlier on that the Governor's Christmas card was our one and only souvenir of our travels; I had forgotten the ditty box. Even now sometimes when I use the box, I think affectionately of those evenings in the Australian bush when I would play the record of 'The Bells of St Mary's'.

It was little more than six months from the time we landed on the Australian shores to the time we set sail again for our native land.

CHAPTER 17

A Return to Cornwall

THE JOURNEY FROM PLYMOUTH TO PENZANCE WAS ONE OF THE greatest thrills of my life.

I felt a lump in my throat as we steamed into Redruth station and I saw the familiar name; but it was an even greater thrill as we slowly steamed out again and passed over the railway arch, under which I had so often played with my little brother Harry, and from which I could now see that beloved row of whitewashed cottages. The one in which I had as an infant lived with my grandparents was in the centre of the row. A tumult of emotions welled up within me as I gazed, then the cottages passed out of sight as the familiar hill blocked the view. The children clamoured for attention, and as I came out of my daydream I made up my mind that I would bring them into Redruth one day while we were on holiday; we would walk into Church town, when I would call at the old cottage and see for myself whether Mr and Mrs Pascoe were still alive and, if they were, I planned to spend a few shillings on some little comforts for them.

Very soon now we caught sight of the sea glinting in the sunlight. How well I remembered all the different landmarks! Could I possibly be the same person, I wondered, as that dirty ragged unkempt child of so long ago that tramped around here with the hurdy-gurdy, and later sang Sankey and Moody hymns? Truly it seemed as if it must have been in another existence.

Now at last we were at Penzance station. As I lifted the children out of the carriage I thought of the last time I had arrived at this very station when I was met by a tall good-looking policeman. This time a kindly middle-aged clergyman awaited us. He came over to us at once and shook hands. 'I knew it must be you by the three little girls,' he said. This good vicar, to whom I had written, not only recommended lodgings but had been kind enough to bring a cab to meet us.

'What street did you live in when you were here as a child?' the vicar asked.

I told him, and blushed as I did so, for somehow I could not dissociate the name of the street from ugly shameful memories. Then I said, truthfully, 'Somehow, I'd like to see it again.'

'Of course you would,' he replied heartily, then added, 'Here it is. We are at the bottom of it now.' I looked out of the cab window, but I felt more pain than pleasure.

Soon we were passing the grey stone building of the school. My joy was reflected on the vicar's own face, for he seemed genuinely pleased that the sight of the school had given me so much pleasure.

The next day I went across to the school and, before calling on the headmistress, I gave myself the pleasure of listening to the familiar hymn being sung at morning prayers, 'Shall we not love thee, Mother dear'.

Later, I took the children over and called on Miss Joyce. 'The vicar told me about you,' she said, 'but I'm afraid I've forgotten you.'

I explained that I had been called Emma Pratt while at her school. Miss Joyce's puzzled look gave way to one of delighted recognition.

'Why, Emma, of course I remember you,' she said. 'I wondered so often what had become of you. We used to feel so dreadfully sorry for you. How well I remember that dreadful old man that used to drag you round with him. We called him 'Fagin,' for he reminded us exactly of the Fagin in *Oliver Twist*.'

'That is an apt description,' I replied.

We chatted for a while and the children came in for a good deal of admiration. 'I should like you to bring the children to tea with me tomorrow at the Pavilion,' Miss Joyce said.

That was a perfect holiday. The little ones revelled in the paddling and bucket and spade work, and when not on the beach, we took walks round the countryside, which brought back a crowd of memories of which I could not talk to the children. I could not discuss my former life at Penzance with my landlady or any other person with whom I came into contact, except Miss Joyce. There was always the possibility that somebody might remember old 'Fagin', as I now think of him, and the little girl that used to accompany him. Not everyone could be trusted to be sympathetic as Miss Joyce was.

I kept the promise I had made to myself and devoted one whole day to an excursion to Redruth. We walked from the station out to Church town. My heart beat with excitement as we passed landmarks that I remembered with affection. I grieved when I encountered anything new which showed change. As the children tripped gaily through a field, the footpath of which I knew would bring us out close to that row of whitewashed cottages and the parish church, I looked eagerly for a certain seat let into a hedge and which, in my infancy, I had known as Lovers' Seat. Harry and I had so often played by it. Now it was missing and my disappointed cry attracted the attention of a lady who was just passing us on the footpath. 'There used to be a seat here, and it's not here any more,' I said aloud.

'Oh, we make progress here as well as in other parts of

the country, you know,' said the lady in a brisk voice that matched her step.

Before I could make a suitable reply she had stepped over the stile and had disappeared from view. I heard later that she was the vicar's wife and not a native, so how could she understand how I felt?

I was thankful that progress had not bereaved me of the row of whitewashed cottages also. These now came into view, together with the tree with its circular stone seat around it, upon which we had so often sat at play. The question now was, should I find Mrs Pascoe and her husband still there alive and well? Even when I had stayed with them about twenty years before they had seemed quite old. I hardly dared to hope I should find them now.

I stood before that beloved little door just as I had done at the age of twelve, when I had arrived footsore and weary after running away from the Pratts. I knocked, and the door opened. A tiny bent figure stood before me and peered up into my face. 'Yes?' she asked.

'Could you tell me,' I said, 'if Mrs Pascoe that used to live here is still living?'

'I am Mrs Pascoe,' she replied with her head shaking a little.

I could hardly keep the tears back as I stooped and kissed that dear wrinkled face. 'And *I* am Emma Smith, or at least I was Emma Smith,' I said.

'Good Lord! Never!' she exclaimed in surprise. Then she said, 'Come in Emma, my dear, do. Are these your children?'

'Yes,' I said proudly, as I drew the shy little ones into that well remembered living-room. 'They are my children, and I've brought them to Penzance for a holiday, and I felt I must look you up again.'

By this time teacups were rattling, and I noticed an old, old man in the chimney corner. 'Can that be Mr Pascoe?' I asked.

'Yes, Emma, my dear. God has been good to us, and we

are still spared to each other,' the dear soul replied, as she poured boiling water on to the tea leaves. 'He is asleep now, and I don't suppose he will wake for some time yet,' she said.

I was so delighted to see my old friends again, and as we sat at tea, I assured Mrs Pascoe again how grateful I had always been to her for taking me in when I arrived at her door unhappy and friendless all those years before.

'Well, Emma, I couldn't have done less,' she said, 'for your dear grandmother was my best friend.'

Then she went on to tell me what I had known before, namely that she had worked for my great-grandmother on the farm where my grandmother grew up as a girl. Later, after both were married and Grandmother's circumstances became so poor, they found themselves next door neighbours, and the bond of friendship between them became very strong.

While the children were finishing their tea, I looked round the room. The few knickknacks that I remembered before as having belonged to my grandmother were still in the places I had remembered them on my previous visit. After tea I took the little ones to the shops where I purchased a few groceries for the old folks. My old friend beamed as she saw what we had brought her, even while protesting that we ought not to have done it. Mr Pascoe was awake now, but, though his wife shouted again and again in his ear who we were and where we came from, the aged man seemed not to be able to understand.

We now bid our old friends 'Goodbye' as it turned out to be for the last time, for I never saw them again.

The next day I wrote to the Sister Superior at Bramshot asking if on our return journey I could bring the children to stay at the Convent for one night, as I was very anxious to show them off to my old friends there. I was bitterly disappointed when her reply came. 'My dear Emma,' she wrote. 'This is a penitentiary, and much as we should like to see your children, such a thing cannot be allowed,' etc., etc.

I felt shocked and bewildered. My reply was, I fear, somewhat bitter, for I told myself it was an awful thing that I should look upon such a place as 'Home', and that I could love a place to which I could not take my children. My reply was as follows:

Dear Sister Superior,
    You are quite right. The Home is a penitentiary. I had forgotten the fact, because you see I had never fully realized it. I was, as you know, so young when I came to you, that I developed a great love for the place, and to me it has always been *Home*. I now realize it is not the sort of place to which I can bring my children, so I will say 'Goodbye', and try to forget you all.
        Yours with love and respect,
            Emma.

This brought another letter from the Sister Superior by return of post, which went as follows:

Dear Emma,
    I have discussed the matter with Sister Kate and the Chaplain. We have decided it would be very nice indeed to see you and your little ones. So *do* come. You can all sleep at the Cottage, one of the dormitories is empty and can be put at your disposal.
        Yours affectionately,
            Clara,
                Sister Superior.

When our time came to leave Penzance, a great longing came over me that we might come here and make it our home. No other county but Cornwall could fill me with the sense of belonging, the feeling of being at home as this my native county did; though of course, as I have already said many times, the Convent at Bramshot was home to me.

176

We now took the train to Bramshot, passing through Plymouth, where my mother lived, without giving her hardly a thought.

As I passed through the Convent gate with my little ones, I felt the proudest woman on earth. What a fuss those sisters made of the children, especially the lay sisters, some of whom I had known since I first arrived there at the age of twelve. Sister Kate, I am sure, was almost as proud of them as if they had indeed been her own grandchildren.

Had we stayed at the Convent longer than one day, I am certain those children would have been hopelessly spoilt. It was amusing the way all these unmarried people would pass good advice upon me as to the best way to bring my family up. I was warned not to let the little dears catch cold, for the sun was not powerful enough yet and the grass might be a trifle damp for their feet. On no account must I let them come out into the sun without their hats, or sunstroke would immediately follow. Was I sure their breakfast eggs were fresh enough? Children's little insides were so soon upset, and so on. Oh, but it was good to be among them all once again, and as I looked at the dear Sister Superior, who still had that habit of drawing her veil tightly round her that I had found so alarming in my young days, I noticed the affectionate gleam in her eyes as she regarded the children, and I wondered how on earth I could ever have stood in such awe of her. The time to bid them farewell came all too quickly for me.

Looking back to this period of my life, I think how true it is that we do not know when we are well off. I am, however, cursed with the spirit of restlessness; something round the corner is always better than what I have now. I began to long intensely to go back to my native county to live. The holiday we had spent at Penzance had increased my natural restlessness, and in time we decided to look for a post near Penzance.

During this restless period, we had a visit one winter's evening from a very smart-looking young trumpeter, who was stationed nearby with his artillery regiment. It turned out to be my youngest half-brother whom I had last seen as a boy of nine, before sailing for Australia. We were delighted to see the boy. He told us that his regiment had been ordered to India for a few years and that he would be quite close to us until they sailed in a few weeks' time. His father thought him too young to go abroad and hoped I would see his commanding officer and beg that he might be exempt from overseas service. I was requested to lay special stress upon the fact that he was his mother's youngest son and that she could not bear to feel he was so far away from her. I promised to do what I could about the matter, but I think the lad himself hoped that my intercession would not carry much weight, for, boy-like, he was all for adventure.

I duly saw the commanding officer, but before I could say very much I was told brusquely that my brother could not be tied to his mother's apron strings all his life, and that it was in the lad's own interest that he went out with his regiment. 'He is highly intelligent,' the Captain said, 'and he should do well. We draw most of our non-commissioned officers from the trumpeters.'

I had failed in my mission, but was proud to hear the manner in which the Captain praised my mother's youngest son.

Little did that captain think, as he spoke, that the day would come when this same boy would hold a high rank as a commissioned officer. He went to India a boy, and came back a man. My mother is justly proud of him and of the way he has worked himself up by one promotion after another. At the time he came to us, however, he was little more than a child, and as I was nineteen years his senior, I very much enjoyed mothering him. He made our home his headquarters while the regiment was there, and as he heard frequently from his father, who was a good letter-writer, I received all the family news. The boy was not aware that I was only a half-sister, and I did not enlighten him. To my children he played the part of a delightful elder brother, and great was their sorrow when the time for parting came.

After his regiment left for India, we kept in touch by letter for some considerable time. I very much enjoyed receiving a letter from him, for they were always interesting and beautifully written. I started to write often to my mother now, but I could never really forget her unnatural treatment in my early days, and after a while I again dropped the correspondence.

Soon after my brother's departure, we made what I shall always feel was one of our biggest mistakes. We obtained a joint post at Penzance and went there to live. We had a cottage on a large estate, where I was to run the private laundry and my husband was to go in the gardens. The estate was one that I had often visited in my singing days as a child, and though I could not remember the village with its pretty cottages very clearly, I remembered the mansion very well indeed.

The owner of the estate was now a widow, and it was to her I had written when we decided to make our home in Penzance. In my young days, this lady's husband was well known for his good works and generosity to the poor. How his estate survived the numerous calls upon his purse must have puzzled many people.

It was with the memory of Mr Penhale's goodness that I now wrote to his widow, telling her I was a native of Cornwall and that I had known her home when I was a child and was now anxious to settle in or near Penzance with my husband and children. Did she, I asked, know of anyone who would employ a gardener? I myself was a trained laundress and could make myself useful in that capacity. Mrs Penhale replied that her private laundress was on the point of giving up on account of her health, and that she had not yet filled her place. She now offered the post to me with a house in the village. My husband, she said, could be given work in the gardens.

Great was my delight when I received this letter. We

now gave notice to leave our present post and very quickly made arrangements for travelling and removal of furniture. Alas, I very soon realized that it was one thing to take two weeks' holiday among the scenes of my childhood, and quite another to live there always. My new employer often entertained visitors and at times the week's laundry was very heavy indeed. It would have been more than some single women could get through in a week, while I was a wife and mother of three children with my own home to run as well as the laundry. I gave satisfaction in my work all right, but at the cost of my own health and children's happiness.

My children, while young, attended my old school. This was two miles distant, but they were pretty hardy and for the most part enjoyed the walking. Miss Joyce took the same interest in them that she had taken in me. She assured me again and again that I had every reason to be proud of them. When duties would permit, I sometimes visited the school, both for old times' sake and also to find out how the children were progressing. When I saw them in class or the playground, I used to compare their neat appearance in white blouses, navy tunics, and neat trimmed hair, to my own unkempt condition while at school.

The village was very pretty and picturesque. The iron railings before our cottage were covered with roses in the summer, and we had a good garden. Most of the villagers attended the local chapel. There was no church nearer than Penzance, two miles away, and though we usually attended church on Sunday, we occasionally joined the other villagers in the chapel.

The first time I did so, I stared around me as a certain memory came back to me. I saw this very same chapel on the occasion of a revival service long ago. I saw an earnest preacher pacing the rostrum pleading, warning and encouraging. I saw a sore-footed beggar girl stumbling out to the penitent form in fear and trembling. I saw again the kindly villagers who had come round to congratulate me on what they called 'being saved'; and as I looked round the chapel now, I wondered vaguely how many members of this same congregation had been present then, and what they would say and think if they knew that I, the new laundress, had been that beggar girl.

It was some time after my first visit to this little chapel when the estate farmer decided to give a barn-dance in honour of his daughter's engagement. All the villagers were invited. I attended the dance, which was held in the old barn, and as I looked round the barn that also brought memories. I said to myself, 'I slept in this barn one night'; and the memory was not a pleasant one.

The present farmer had only been there for a few years, so I knew he was not the same man who had given Pratt permission for us to sleep there on that occasion so many years before. I think if it had been the same kindly man I should have been tempted to make myself known to him as the beggar child he once took pity on. As it was, nobody knew or guessed what thoughts and memories were crowding into my mind, though one or two people remarked that I looked more as if I was attending a funeral than a dance.

We had been living at Penzance about two years when my husband and I both fell ill with influenza. I had to nurse my husband who seemed in danger of pneumonia, so I could not take to my bed. My work was sent to a steam laundry for the time being, however, so I was just left with my home, husband and children to look after. Even these homely duties can seem too much when one is ill.

The influenza left me very depressed. I could not shake it off. It persisted long after I had returned to the laundry, and after some weeks a collapse came and I suffered a severe nervous breakdown. We had a very good family doctor, who ordered me to a private nursing home. This proved so expensive that after two weeks I left still ill. I turned against my husband completely for the time being, and even my love for and interest in my children was not strong enough to make me wish to live.

I partially recovered, but had many relapses, and if it were not for the fact that my good doctor let me pour out my troubles (real and imaginary) to him again and again, I think I should have lost my reason completely.

Now for some years past I had had a recurring dream which troubled me much at times, so real did it seem. I would dream that I was an inmate of a convent; the convent itself was never clear in the dream, but I was, or could have been, supremely happy if it were not for the knowledge that somewhere in the background I had a husband and children. There I would be in the atmosphere I most loved and among friends who knew, loved, and understood me; yet I would be yearning for the family to which I could not get access. I would awake from the dream with an awful feeling of strain and clutch my little ones tight, so glad would I feel that it had only been 'that dream again'.

I told my doctor a little of my life story during the many interviews I had with him; and once when I had been more depressed than usual and lost so much weight through lack of food, he suggested it might be a good thing if I went to the Convent at Bramshot for a holiday. 'I am sure it will do you a whole lot of good,' he said. I was not in a fit state to make any arrangements, so I languidly replied, 'If the train comes to my bedside I'll go, but I could not write a letter to save my life.' 'I'll see to all that,' the doctor replied, and added, 'By all you have told me of the place, I should say it was the very place for you now.'

Before my breakdown I was a keen churchwoman, but at the time I fell ill I completely lost my faith. I could believe in nothing.

Soon after the doctor had written to Bramshot, I was on my way thither. I was so weak I could hardly walk, but somehow I got over the journey. It was good to be with old friends again. They were kind and patient with me and I felt safe. Even there, for a while, I could do nothing much but weep, while my physical state was such that when I sat down I could not get out of the chair again without help. However, I very soon regained strength and at any rate wept less, though I could not be said to have attained a cheerful outlook. The sisters did not insist upon my attendance at chapel, and for this I was grateful.

One day I had a strong presentiment that my eldest girl was ill. In distress I wrote to the doctor for news, feeling pretty certain that I could rely on more accurate information from him than I could expect to get from my husband. The doctor replied at once to the effect that my fear was justified. Mary had received a blow on the kidney, while at play in the school grounds, and she was now under his care. 'Do not worry,' he wrote, 'for I am attending her, and a neighbour is popping in and out. I insist that you stay where you are, until I give you permission to return.'

I sought out Sister Kate and took the doctor's letter to read. 'Yes, Emma,' she said. 'I also have heard from your doctor, and he insists that you stay here for some time. In fact, he suggests that we now give you a little work to do.'

'My dream, Sister, my dream, ' I moaned. 'Don't Emma,' Sister Kate replied in a troubled voice, for I had often spoken to her of my recurring dream and she knew how it had always haunted me. 'We shall only keep you until you are really well,' she went on, and added, 'My dear child, we shall only be too glad to return you to your family when you are fit to go.'

I was not in a fit frame of mind to see the sense of her argument. All I knew was that go I must, now at once before the Convent swallowed me up for good.

When I knew Sister Kate was in the refectory at dinner, I went to my room and packed my case. Then, without saying 'Goodbye' to anyone except the old cottage sister, to whom I had confided my fears, I walked out of the Convent Cottage carrying my case. Sister Bessie came as far as the gate. I kissed my old friend and said, 'Give my love to Sister Kate and thank her for everything. Beg her not to be angry at the way I am leaving, for I know she will never give me permission to go, and I can't forget that dream.' 'All right, Emma, I know Sister Kate will understand,' Sister Bessie said, and added, 'I think you are quite right to go.'

I set out on my return journey far from well, but all the same a great deal stronger than when I came. Rest, good food, and above all the comings and going of old and dear friends to talk to had had a wonderful effect, and it was a very different mother who returned to her family from the one who had left it a couple of weeks or so previously. Even making up my mind to return home, wrong though it undoubtedly was, had had a tonic effect upon me.

My doctor was not angry, though he had every right to be. His understanding of human nature was greater than his love of authority. I must here place on record that I have never since then been troubled with that recurring dream.

On the way home I was seized suddenly with one of those overwhelming presentiments that seemed to spring upon me in my younger days, but which never seem to come upon me now I am older. All at once I was convinced, without the shadow of a doubt, that my mother was in my home. This was all the more surprising in that I had not written to her for a very long time, for in those days I was very changeable in my attitude towards her. Sometimes the bitterness left by my early life was so great that I would stop writing; and if a brother or sister wrote asking me to send a letter to her, I would curtly write back to the effect that my mother was nothing to me, and that in fact I had no relatives. I would then be left alone for a further period of a year or perhaps two. Then would come the inevitable day when I would once again remind myself that 'after all she is my mother'. At these times I recalled the homely sitting-room and atmosphere of her home as we knew it when visiting her before sailing for Australia. Then I would start corresponding again.

This presentiment that had seized upon me in the train was after one of these long periods of silence. I did not even know if Mother was living at the same address. Yet as I have said, I was now certain she was in my home. I was not at all pleased about it. I wanted to be alone with my family when I returned. I had sent a wire to my husband, telling him I was on my way and the time of arrival.

When he met me, his greeting was, 'You've got a visitor.'

'I know,' I replied wearily, 'it's my mother.'

I was so tired after my journey, for I was still far from strong, and now I was exasperated to think I should have to turn to and work extra to entertain a mother I did not want, and had not invited. And yet – after all – when I met her stout puffing figure coming up the hill to meet me – I was glad to see her, and I am bound to admit that her presence gave the cottage a very homely atmosphere.

Mother said, 'I've had words with Father, so I've walked out and thought I would come to see you. I didn't tell him where I was going.'

'Well, for goodness' sake, won't he worry?' I asked.

'Well, I expect he did for a few hours,' she replied, 'but he will be here any time now, for I can't bear to be away from him. And when I found your home was so comfortable, I thought it would be nice for us both to stay here for a holiday; so I sent him a wire, asking him to come.'

I was much too tired to argue about this cool remark, and at the time it was made we were still walking towards the cottage and I had not yet seen Mary about whose health I had been worrying; this blotted other things from my mind. We had now reached home and I was soon reunited to my family, and it was not long before Mary recovered from her illness.

My stepfather came almost at once when he received Mother's wire, and we were now a houseful. While she had been awaiting his arrival, Mother told me, with many chuckles, that her husband had left her once while in a bad temper, and had gone all the way to Glasgow to get a job at the docks. Three days later he returned, saying, 'I couldn't stay away from you, Maud.' 'And when he said that, he nearly hugged me to death,' she said proudly. I smiled, somewhat bitterly; there was no doubt, I thought enviously that Mother and her husband were certainly in love and always had been, whatever their individual faults were.

They stayed with us for two weeks, and I must admit their company did us all good. Mother made herself useful too. She is a good cook, and none knows better how to prepare those special dishes so beloved by the natives of Cornwall.

For a while after my mother left us, things seemed to improve. I was brighter and better in every way than I had been for some long time past. I was able to carry on with my laundry-work and occasionally I was able to go for sea bathes and picnicking with the girls, and altogether we were for a time quite a happy family.

Alas, in time I began to feel ill internally and an operation was advised. I was gravely ill and it was touch and go whether I should recover or not. I was more than willing to die, for I felt I wanted rest from these recurring bouts of depression. I feared life far more than I feared death.

The operation was successful and I did recover physically, but again the depression had me in its grip. One night I took fifty aspirin tablets, feeling certain that that would end it all. I went to sleep and awoke later with my heart thumping so madly that I was certain that this now was to be the end. Then I was violently sick. When I got out of bed I could not stand. I had to crawl to the bathroom on hands and knees. In the morning my doctor was sent for, and failing to get any sense out of what I replied to his questions, he decided to call in Dr White.

Dr White promptly certified me, and before long I was being whisked off to the nearest mental hospital. By the time I reached the hospital I had become a little deaf, but sensible enough to realize what had taken place, and I was overcome with horror and despair. As the car drove through those big gates, I could almost imagine the words painted above them, 'Abandon hope all ye who enter here.' This was much worse than dying, I thought, for it would be a living death. I should for the rest of my life be conscious that I was the mother of three children, yet never be able to see them or perhaps even hear anything of them, for I really believed I should lose touch with all that I had known in my former life.

A faint glimmer of hope, however, stirred in me after I found myself in a ward that looked much the same as any other hospital ward with its flowers on tables down the centre. The ward sister had a bright pleasing face, and when she found I could talk rationally she gave up a little of her time to help and comfort me. 'The doctor will be on his round in the morning, though your nerves must be in a pretty bad state for you to have done such a silly thing. Did your doctor know you had taken all those aspirins?'

'No,' I replied, 'I didn't want him to know.'

'Well, anyhow, you had better cheer up and look forward to going home again,' she said, 'for if you keep crying like you are now, you will be kept here all the longer.'

The kindly day sister went off duty, and a very different sister came on in her place. The very way she wore her cap frightened me. As the patients who had been up all day came to bed, some of them making queer gruesome noises, I thought I really should go mad. I wanted to jump out of bed and scream, 'Let me out! Let me out!' How I restrained myself I do not know. I think it was the night sister's cap worn low on her forehead that made me afraid to move. There was not one wink of sleep for me that night. The horrifying thought that I had been certified, that I was here among the mentally afflicted, not knowing when I should see my family again! Never was daylight more welcome, and glad I was indeed to see the kind face of the day sister once more.

Dr Duncan came on his rounds, and as he came near

my bed with his stethoscope ready to examine me, I cried out, 'Doctor, I'm not mad.'

'I can see you're not,' the Doctor replied, and added, 'We shall want your bed for those that are.'

Oh what a blessed relief those words brought me! I now made the best of a bad job, and took an interest in the other patients. I wrote letters to my husband and children; also to our good family doctor, explaining about the aspirins.

I was very thankful to receive his reply, for I had been afraid that he would now wash his hands of me, and I deeply valued his professional friendship, both on my own and my children's account. He wrote, 'You are now in the hands of the doctors at the mental hospital, who, as soon as they are assured of your sanity, will release you. When this happens, I hope you will keep well, but if you should need further medical advice I shall always be pleased to give it.'

Three weeks later I passed before the Committee and left the hospital with my husband, who had come to fetch me. Now, added to my other troubles, real or imaginary, was the awful thought that I had been 'certified'. The word kept beating on my brain like a hammer – 'You've been certified! You've been certified!' On and on it went when I was alone in my laundry (for I always got my job back). So much did this thought now play on my mind that I made a further attempt upon my life, this time with sleeping tablets which I had procured from a chemist who did not know me. This time I was certain my troubles would come to an end. If the thought of my children being left motherless bothered me at all, I firmly banished it from my mind, telling myself that they would all be better off without me and under the care of those who were more sane and balanced than I was. This attempt also failed. I had taken eleven tablets, very thoughtfully leaving one on the dressing table, so that my doctor could identify the poison that had killed me, and (so I thought) save everyone a lot of work.

I was violently sick and ill, but still living, when that

poor long-suffering doctor visited me the following morning. He looked at the remaining tablet and said, 'You should certainly have died if you took eleven of these, that is if they are what I think they are and, incidentally, I have *never* known anyone taking these tablets to be sick.' Walking over to my bedroom window, he stood looking out thoughtfully for a while, then he said, 'You know, you are not meant to die. You have some work to do.'

These words stuck in my mind, and from that time onwards I made no more attempts upon my life. The words 'You have been certified' were now replaced by the doctor's words 'You have got some work to do.' I pulled myself together in earnest.

Epilogue

THE EVENTS I HAVE RECORDED IN THE LAST FEW PAGES WERE spread over a matter of years. We lived for nine years at Penzance, during which time I was up and down physically and mentally. When ill, I was placed on the panel for a week or two, the certificate being marked 'nervous debility'. I would return to my laundry as soon as I felt a little better, only to get ill again shortly. During the same period my children grew up and did very well indeed at school. Two of them won scholarships to the secondary school, and the third sat for an extrance exam and succeeded in getting a place, for which we paid. The time came when the eldest girl left school and took up what was to prove a very successful career.

Then the Second World War broke out. I now felt called upon to do some kind of war work. I joined the W.R.N.S. and for some months was extremely happy in my work and in the companionship of my fellow-workers, male and female.

One cold winter's day we were suddenly informed that the King was to pay a visit to the barracks that afternoon, and we were to be lined up in the parade ground by two-thirty; the King was expected at 3 p.m. It was certainly a wonderful experience to behold one's king so close, and I would not have missed the opportunity for anything; but it was three-thirty before we were dismissed. The weather was so intensely cold that I seemed to be frozen to the spot. I felt ill and could hardly walk back into the barracks.

I could not leave my bed the next day. The naval doctor visited me and ordered me to hospital, for I had a touch of pneumonia.

When I was better again I returned to duty; but my work, coupled with drilling exercises, was now more than I could cope with, so I put in for my discharge. My officer did her best to keep me, but I knew that I could not possibly cope with both home and barrack life, so I succeeded in getting an honourable discharge. I missed the companionship greatly and shall always look back upon those few months as one of the happiest periods of my life.

I think it is time now to bring my narrative to a close. I hope my readers have been both interested and sympathetic.

I will just state briefly that all three of my daughters turned out well. One of the twins, Ann, followed her elder sister's footsteps and chose the same career in which she is doing splendidly. We are very proud of her achievements. She is doing a real good work in the world. Her twin sister, Susan, after serving for a few years in the W.A.A.F., fell in love and is happily married. She now has a boy and a girl. Unhappily, we are all scattered and see very little of each other.

We are many miles away again now from my mother's home, but I keep in touch with her also, for, as I have said at the beginning of my story, I have learnt to forgive and have grown more tolerant.

I should end my life story on a very happy note if I could honestly record the fact that I have grown so well-balanced mentally that nothing now upsets or worries me. Such, however, is not the case. I am easily worried and upset over certain things, and for this reason as much as for others, I am anxious to find a little cottage somewhere in Cornwall with a bit of ground upon which we can grow vegetables and flowers. It would be a great thrill to me if my dream cottage had a view of both the sun rising and the sunset, for the sun rising fills me with hope, and the sunset fills me with peace.